Chemistories

Written and illustrated by
Maya Mourshed

DEDICATION

To my mother and grandmother for their infinite support.

And to all who see the potential in the very miniscule.

A MESSAGE FROM
THE AUTHOR/ILLUSTRATOR

When I was eight years old, I stumbled across a periodic table in a library book. It captivated me. I absorbed the glorious chart of all 118 chemical elements that make up our world, from hydrogen to oganesson. Each element square contained a two-letter symbol and numbers to represent the element's atomic mass and protons. I wondered what these numbers and letters meant, so I delved more deeply into understanding how the periodic table works. (You can see a copy of the periodic table on page 4-5.) I discovered how each element is used in real life and how groups of elements are related.

I began to imagine what would happen if each element had a life of its own: *What would these elements say? What would their personalities be? What would they do every day?* Because I love creative writing, I began drafting stories about how I imagined the elements behaving.

This book is a collection of the stories and poems I created over three years. Some of this creative work started as short-story contest entries that I elaborated on and refined for this book. Some pieces initially began as a school assignment, and then I took them further on my own time. Throughout this journey, I've tried to combine ideas and concepts that may seem like they don't go together at first. For example, in reality, elements are nonliving, but I've brought them to life through this work. I've expanded on the stories by adding my own drawings to the book.

Creative writing and science are often viewed as unrelated, but I'd like to change that. Chemistry is the foundation of all my stories and poems in this collection. I hope readers will feel the same joy and fascination I felt when I first saw the periodic table. And who knows? Maybe this book will spark your interest in chemistry, too.

Yours in Chemistry,
Maya Mourshed

PERIODIC TABLE OF CONTENTS

PART ONE

Curious Chemistry Chronicles

INTRODUCING ... THE PERIODIC TABLE

This is the periodic table, an icon and the basis of chemistry. Scientists use it to organize *elements* and predict their properties. Elements are made of tiny particles called *atoms*. Think of it this way: if you were an atom, your family would be an element. So, if you made a list of all the families in your neighborhood, that list would be the periodic table.

At first glance, the periodic table may look like a strange sequence of letters, numbers, names, and measurements—all fitted into squares. But I like to imagine that behind each square is a life. Each element has its own personality, its own voice, its own being.

These are their stories.

THE PERIODIC TABLE OF ELEMENTS

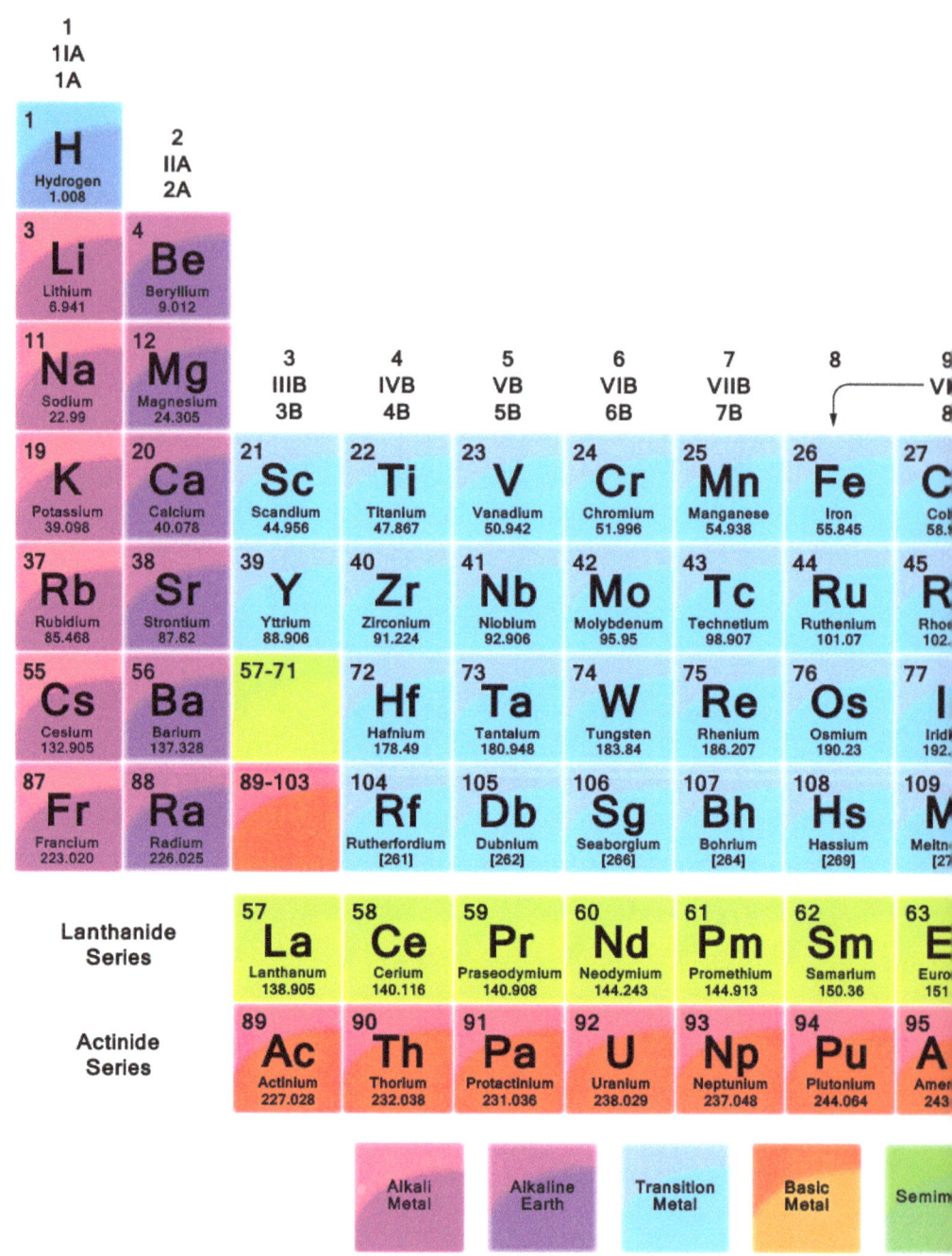

4

							18 VIIIA 8A
							2 **He** Helium 4.003
	13 IIIA 3A	14 IVA 4A	15 VA 5A	16 VIA 6A	17 VIIA 7A		
	5 **B** Boron 10.811	6 **C** Carbon 12.011	7 **N** Nitrogen 14.007	8 **O** Oxygen 15.999	9 **F** Fluorine 18.998	10 **Ne** Neon 20.180
10 ↓	11 IB 1B	12 IIB 2B	13 **Al** Aluminum 26.982	14 **Si** Silicon 28.086	15 **P** Phosphorus 30.974	16 **S** Sulfur 32.066	17 **Cl** Chlorine 35.453	18 **Ar** Argon 39.948

10	11 IB 1B	12 IIB 2B	13 IIIA 3A	14 IVA 4A	15 VA 5A	16 VIA 6A	17 VIIA 7A	18 VIIIA 8A
Ni Nickel 8.693	29 **Cu** Copper 63.546	30 **Zn** Zinc 65.38	31 **Ga** Gallium 69.723	32 **Ge** Germanium 72.631	33 **As** Arsenic 74.922	34 **Se** Selenium 78.971	35 **Br** Bromine 79.904	36 **Kr** Krypton 83.789
Pd Palladium 06.42	47 **Ag** Silver 107.868	48 **Cd** Cadmium 112.414	49 **In** Indium 114.818	50 **Sn** Tin 118.711	51 **Sb** Antimony 121.760	52 **Te** Tellurium 127.6	53 **I** Iodine 126.904	54 **Xe** Xenon 131.294
Pt Platinum 95.085	79 **Au** Gold 196.967	80 **Hg** Mercury 200.592	81 **Tl** Thallium 204.383	82 **Pb** Lead 207.2	83 **Bi** Bismuth 208.980	84 **Po** Polonium [208.982]	85 **At** Astatine 209.987	86 **Rn** Radon 222.018
Ds nstadtium [281]	111 **Rg** Roentgenium [280]	112 **Cn** Copernicium [285]	113 **Nh** Nihonium [286]	114 **Fl** Flerovium [289]	115 **Mc** Moscovium [286]	116 **Lv** Livermorium [293]	117 **Ts** Tennessine [294]	118 **Og** Oganesson [294]

	65 **Tb** Terbium 158.925	66 **Dy** Dysprosium 162.500	67 **Ho** Holmium 164.930	68 **Er** Erbium 167.259	69 **Tm** Thulium 168.934	70 **Yb** Ytterbium 173.055	71 **Lu** Lutetium 174.967
Gd Iolinium 57.25							
Cm urium 47.070	97 **Bk** Berkelium 247.070	98 **Cf** Californium 251.080	99 **Es** Einsteinium [254]	100 **Fm** Fermium 257.095	101 **Md** Mendelevium 258.1	102 **No** Nobelium 259.101	103 **Lr** Lawrencium [262]

nmetal   Halogen   Noble Gas   Lanthanide   Actinide

ODE TO CHEMISTRY

Since the age of eight,
The periodic table beckoned me inside it:
A dazzling, grand list
Of all 118 chemical elements
Ever known to humankind
From the beginning of time.

I cross its every group and period,
Visiting all the elements' families,
On a quest to memorize each
Chemical symbol,
Atomic number,
Usage and property,
Imagining that one day
In front of the whole world
I would recite this list
From top to bottom,
From hydrogen to oganesson.

I jump from hydrogen to helium,
Receiving an alkali metal burst from lithium
And an alkaline earth metal boost from beryllium
To brittle nonmetals,

Reactive halogens,
And inert noble gases.
I trek through the transition metals,
Passing from iron to cobalt to nickel to copper.
Leaping from barium into the lanthanides,
I run over to lutetium,
Continuing on my merry way
Until I reach radium,
Bouncing into the actinides until lawrencium diminishes me.
On I crawl through the artificial last elements,
Livermorium, tennessine, then—oganesson.
My trip is complete.

I absorb the elements,
Developing plans
To become the Marie Curie of the future.
Even though my classmates
Doubt me for this deep passion,
I continue to pursue my dreams,
Identifying every element
In everything I see or touch.

The periodic table
Remains my closest friend,
And my strong love of chemistry
Continues to glow bright,
Illuminating my mind
With its beauty.

THE ATOM

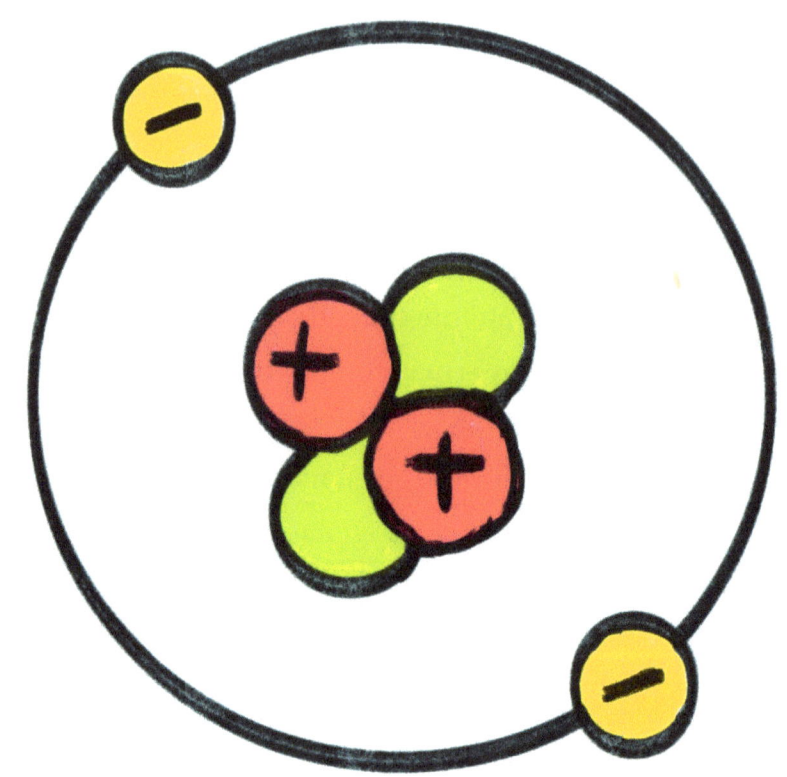

+ = PROTON

= NEUTRON

- = ELECTRON

WHAT ARE ATOMS AND ELEMENTS?

Everything in the world is made up of tiny particles called atoms. Because atoms are so small, scientists can only see them with a special device called an *electron microscope*. Atoms have three parts: *protons*, *neutrons*, and *electrons*. The protons, which are positively charged, and the neutrons, which have a charge of zero, are in the atom's center in a place called the *nucleus*. The electrons, which are negatively charged, orbit quickly around the nucleus.

Most atoms have an equal number of protons and electrons—it's kind of like two magnets that attract each other. Since the protons and electrons cancel each other out, the charge of most atoms is neutral or zero.

Something that is made of only one kind of atom is called an element. So far, 118 elements have been discovered and depicted in the periodic table.[1]

[1] To learn how to read the periodic table, see page 113.

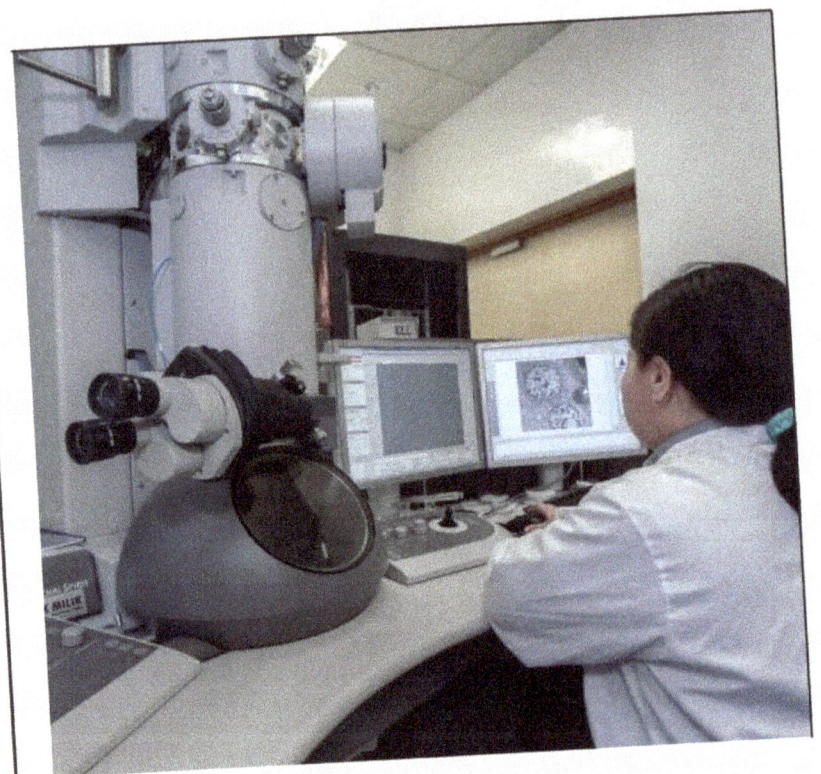

Electron microscopes use electron beams as
sources of light to create images of atoms.

WHO IS ELEMENT 119?

(An Ununennium Story)

(UN-un-NEN-nee-yum)

Inside the Lab ...

R.T. Fishul rarely spent time with people, but she always had time for her chemical elements. She was a brilliant scientist who had turned down offers from universities and companies so that she could dedicate herself to the chemistry innovations she believed mattered most to advancing the world. Using all her savings, she turned her basement into a sophisticated lab and had even built her own cyclotron.

And what is a cyclotron, you might ask? A cyclotron is a machine that is *supposed* to fuse two or more atoms of different elements to create an entirely new element—but this rarely works. The cyclotron is a particle accelerator that charges positive particles of one element and then shoots them at another element with a beam.[2] Scientists had been conducting trials to fuse elements for the past twenty years, but only four new elements have been created to date.

Only a total of 118 chemical elements have been discovered in the world so far, thought R.T. *I can do better than that. I know I can discover a new element—maybe even more than one. I'll keep trying with my cyclotron, no matter how long it takes.*

R.T. was determined to have a successful trial. "I'll fuse two elements in my cyclotron to create something new. Something like ... a green energy source."

R.T.'s basement lab had black walls with green patterns reminiscent of a circuit board. Her computer sat on top of her desk. Gray filing cabinets stored her important scientific documents. The

---

[2] To learn more about how cyclotrons work, see page 121.

lab also featured test tubes and flasks filled with colorful liquids. In the middle of it all—in its full glory—stood the grand, cylindrical cyclotron. It was a few inches taller than R.T. herself and ten times her width.

The cyclotron's blue and yellow wires traversed over its gray exterior. On one side was a small panel that controlled the two inner D-shaped magnets that forcefully blasted the atoms.

"Good morning, cyclotron!" rang R.T.'s voice in the quiet of the lab. She loved that she was alone with no one to distract her.

R.T. had always felt more comfortable around inanimate objects than human beings. Inanimate objects were predictable— she knew what they were designed to do, and they did so reliably. In contrast, humans were unpredictable and had volatile emotions that exhausted R.T. Dealing with humans was akin to climbing Mount Everest. Twice.

R.T. got straight to work. She kept a scientific journal that logged every trial to combine atoms, as well as her observations of each one. She had conducted fifty trials so far, focusing on fusing the elements bismuth and krypton.

The damage-resistance properties of bismuth should combine perfectly with krypton's energy abilities, R.T. thought to herself. But, for some reason, the fusion wasn't working no matter how hard R.T. tried.

"Time to begin again!" said R.T., grabbing a new journal.

It had a solid black cover made of thick cardboard. The front read: OBSERVATIONS, just as all her other ones had. R.T.'s well-worn journals were her most prized possessions. *Flip* went the pages of R.T.'s journal. *Click* went her blue ink pen.

"A fresh page. A new start," she whispered to herself.

Whenever she felt adrift, R.T. anchored herself in the seven steps of the scientific method.

1. Observation:
My past 50 trials with the cyclotron have failed in fusing bismuth and krypton.

R.T. had a hypothesis that the combination of these two elements could create a new energy source that would replace fossil fuels. It would be element 119, representing a massive chemistry breakthrough beyond the 118 elements that currently existed. Even though it hadn't been discovered yet, the element had already been given a name by the chemistry field, based on the Latin root for the number 119: *ununennium* (UN-un-NEN-nee-yum).

She paused to think …

2. Question:
Why have all my past trials failed?

And then she wrote …

Just like Thomas Edison and his repeated attempts to create the lightbulb, I have learned 50 things that didn't work, which means I haven't failed once. This gets me fifty times closer to finding out what will work.

Following the usual steps of the scientific method, she continued …

3. Hypothesis:

The magnetic force isn't strong enough for fusion, or the speed of the atom going toward the target needs to be faster.

4. Prediction:

If I increase the magnets' force at the start of the trial, such that krypton accelerates faster toward bismuth, I will be able to successfully fuse bismuth and krypton.

With her prediction in mind, R.T. walked over to the cyclotron and adjusted the voltage of the two D-shaped magnets. She then took a deep breath before starting her fifty-first trial of fusing bismuth and krypton.

R.T. turned toward the periodic table dashboard on the wall, which acted as an element dispenser akin to a vending machine. Not for snacks, of course. For chemical elements!

R.T. knew that each element square had a button. However, she did *not* know that behind each button were *actual living* families of atoms of different elements.

Inside the Periodic Table ...

Scientists had always mistakenly thought that atoms were nonliving. Atoms didn't need nutrients. They didn't breathe. They didn't have cells. They didn't reproduce, either. However, in reality, the atoms *have* been doing all those things for centuries ... in secret.

Whenever scientists studied them, the atoms froze so they could fool the scientists into believing they were nonliving. Atoms had a long-held fear that scientists would treat them like lab rats, poking them with a needle or prodding them with a pair of tweezers. Scientists would likely do all sorts of awful experiments on atoms if they knew that atoms were living. Think of surgery minus the anesthesia. Oh, how dreadful that would feel! So Hydrogen, the first element of the periodic table and leader of the atoms, had led all of his peers to commit that they would pretend to be nonliving in the presence of humans.

Each atom family consisted of clones, similar to bees in a beehive. For example, all the bismuth atoms lived together behind the "bismuth button." They all looked the same. They talked the same. They reacted the same. And the atoms kept to themselves, only engaging with their own element. Each element family not only looked different but also had its own personality profile. The Bismuths had vocal and dominant personalities, whereas the Kryptons were inert and quiet.

All the Bismuths had rainbow-colored hair that curled in square spirals, with the letters "Bi" imprinted on their chest and the number 83 levitating above their head. In contrast, all the Kryptons were bright blue in color, had dark, side-swept hair that partially concealed their eyes, and had the letters "Kr" on their chest and the number 36 floating above them.

So, what did the families do inside the periodic table all day, you might wonder? Each element family spent its time chatting with each other, learning chemistry, and spying on R.T. The latter had proven to be particularly acute for the Bismuths and Kryptons of late, because R.T. kept using them in trial after trial. Into her cyclotron they'd go—whether they wanted to or not.

"Isn't it horrible!?" Bismuth Beth shouted. "Every one of R.T.'s trials makes one of our family members disappear!"

Her little brother, Bismuth Ben, shuddered. "Yeah, and if she continues to do the trials, things could get even worse for us! We might—become extinct or something!"

The Bismuths weren't the only element family anxious about R.T.'s trials making their family size decrease exponentially over the past weeks.

"Looks like R.T. isn't taking the hint," sighed Krypton Kate, from within another element square. "She will never be able to fuse us because we don't want to be fused. It's a nightmare."

Krypton's mother, Krypton Kora, whispered, "Hopefully we don't end up in there. We would vanish like our family members already have."

R.T.'s fusion trials had forced the Bismuths and Kryptons into awkward—and ultimately fatal— situations. They had hoped from R.T.'s dejected reactions that she would stop her experiments. After all, she had gone through fifty failed trials. How many blunders could one person make before shifting course? But here R.T. was again, about to embark on the fifty-first trial. Which meant that more Bismuths and Kryptons would be sucked into the cyclotron and gone forever. A wave of grief fell over the atoms whenever one of their loved ones departed.

The Bismuths and Kryptons watched in dismay as R.T. pressed their buttons. *REEEEE-RT!* Suddenly, a tube shot up into both element squares—a signal that it was time for one member of each of the families to leave.

"Looks like we spoke too soon," said Krypton Kora.

Bismuth Beth and Krypton Kate felt a vacuum pressure immediately force them down a slide into the cyclotron. *FWOOSH!*

At the Entrance of the Cyclotron ...

Bismuth Beth blinked her eyes and slowly rose to her feet as she absorbed her new surroundings. Krypton Kate emitted a panicked shriek as she lay splayed on the ground.

"Who are *you*?" asked Bismuth Beth, taking in the blue creature in front of her.

"Wait, who are *you*?" asked Krypton Kate, startled by the multicolored figure before her.

"I'm Bismuth Beth," "I'm Krypton Kate," they blurted simultaneously.

"I get it. You live in the same periodic table that I live in. We have no time to waste!" Bismuth Beth declared. "We know how this story is going to end. R.T. is going to fail in her experiment again, and you and I will disappear forever!"

"M—my family's been watching R.T., too," said Krypton Kate, shivering. "I don't want to fade away like my other family members did!"

"What do you think we should do to get R.T. to stop these experiments?"

"I don't know!" wailed Krypton Kate in despair. "I'm scared."

"Think! R.T. is getting ready to turn on the cyclotron!" Bismuth Beth shouted, glancing through the glass pane of the cyclotron's entrance. "We have *minutes*—no, *seconds* to solve this problem," she said, pacing back and forth. "Could we jump out of the cyclotron?"

"Nope. We might get squished."

"What if we break the cyclotron so it stops working?" said Bismuth Beth. "Nah, we're too small to do something like that." Then she gasped—an idea taking shape in her mind. "I've got a plan. What if we *reveal* ourselves and then ask R.T. to stop?"

"*Uhhh* . . . what do you mean by *reveal* ourselves? Show her that we're living?" asked Krypton Kate. "We've protected our secret for . . . forever!"

"We're running out of time here," said Bismuth Beth. "R.T.'s almost done adjusting the two magnets in the cyclotron—we're doomed!"

"This decision is bigger than us alone," said Krypton Kate. "All the elements of the periodic table have agreed on freezing in front of humans since the creation of the periodic table by Dmitri Mendeleev.[3] We can't simply *undo* the agreement without consulting all the elements and—"

Bismuth Beth had stopped listening. Instead, she waved her little hands to attract R.T.'s attention as she stood at the cyclotron's entrance. Bismuth Beth stomped her feet as hard as she could, *tip-tap, tip-tap, tip!*

And then it happened . . .

R.T. saw Bismuth Beth—and let out a piercing shriek.

---

[3] Learn more about Dmitri Mendeleev on page 118.

Human Meets Atoms …

What on earth? R.T. took several steps closer to the window pane at the cyclotron's entrance, rubbing her eyes as she stared through the glass. Did she really see something small waving and stomping at her? Was it a hallucination? Had she forgotten to clean her glasses this morning? Or not gotten enough sleep last night?

R.T. grabbed a magnifying glass from her desk and pressed it against the cyclotron's window. What she saw was a tiny figure waving its arms at her. What could this possibly be? A speck of dust? An ant that had learned to stand up? An atom? An ATOM?

R.T. took big gulps of air to prevent herself from hyperventilating.

Just as she had begun to think she was seeing things, R.T. heard tiny, high-pitched voices arguing.

"Now look at what you've done! She *spotted* us!" said one voice.

"Yeah, *that was the point*! Would you rather disappear forever?" said the other.

The two figures pointed their tiny fingers at her.

Ahh … poor R.T. Fishul. Can you blame her for tossing her magnifying glass over her shoulder and collapsing onto the floor? There she was, curled up into a ball, shivering, her head tucked between her knees. What would you do if you saw two tiny creatures like Bismuth Beth and Krypton Kate? You might have had a panic attack, too!

R.T. finally raised her head from her position. *Is something wrong with me? Should I call 911?* R.T. wondered.

But R.T. was a scientist through and through. That meant she was curious. She looked up at the painting on her wall: her silver-haired grandmother, Benny Fishul. The sight of her face broke R.T. out of her panic attack.

What would my grandmother do? R.T. channeled her inner Benny Fishul. *I just saw tiny creatures inside the cyclotron. I have to stay curious and find out more about them even though I'm scared. I should just follow the science wherever it leads.*

R.T. took small steps towards the cyclotron, and then picked up her magnifying glass, ready to take a closer look.

R.T. looked straight at one of the tiny creatures, who appeared to be waving her hand. The creature then spoke. "Allow us to introduce ourselves. I'm Bismuth Beth, and she is Krypton Kate. We're both atoms."

Atoms? thought R.T. *Alive? Impossible.*

Bismuth Beth continued. "Although you humans think that atoms aren't alive, we are. We live in the periodic table. And we've been watching you make our family members disappear whenever you put them in the cyclotron. You have to stop because you're *killing* us!"

R.T. broke out of her trance and spoke. "W—what do you mean you're alive? Atoms are nonliving. They don't need nutrients, don't breathe, don't have cells, and don't reproduce," she stated defiantly.

Krypton Kate joined the conversation. "This is exactly what we mean. Humans' understanding of atoms is so limited. Of course we breathe, eat, and reproduce. I live with my family inside the periodic table. So do all of the other element families. We've just hidden our capabilities from humans by freezing whenever they're present."

R.T. collapsed in a chair. What she was hearing had challenged everything she had ever known about chemistry.

R.T. shook her head. "H—how could this possibly be true? It's been hundreds of years since the periodic table was invented! How come all scientists from the past decades never knew that you were alive?"

"Are you crazy?" burst out Bismuth Beth. "If we told you humans that we were alive, we'd all get treated like guinea pigs! Scientists do crazy experiments on them that you'd never do to a human! Do you *really* think we would want that to happen to us? *Hmm*?"

Krypton Kate nodded in agreement.

R.T. crossed her arms, regaining her confidence. "This new information is incredible!" She took a deep breath and reached for her journal. "Everything that I've ever learned in my entire academic career—from my university professors, from my textbooks—all of it states that atoms aren't alive. The entire foundation of the chemistry field is based on this one fact: that atoms are nonliving."

She stood, pacing back and forth in front of the cyclotron. As she paced, she heard whispers from the atoms.

"Do you think she's okay? Why's she talking to herself?"

"Maybe she's thinking. Humans just don't know how to navigate new information as well as we atoms do."

R.T. stopped and stared at a picture of a silver-haired woman on the wall.

"Who is that?" asked Krypton Kate.

The question broke R.T. out of her thinking. "This is a picture of my grandmother, Benny Fishul," R.T. stated. "She was a physicist who inspired me to get into science, even when my own parents doubted me. No one was more delighted than her when I got my PhD in chemistry. We always did our experiments together until she passed away. I can only imagine what she would say if she could hear the three of us talking right now."

"Well, what *would* she say?" asked Bismuth Beth.

R.T. immediately responded. "She would tell me to follow the science wherever it leads, no matter if I like it or not."

"Do you know *why* we've revealed ourselves to you?" asked Bismuth Beth.

"And not to any other scientist?" added Krypton Kate.

"Please, tell me," answered R.T. "Why *did* you reveal yourselves to me?"

"Because you're doing something impossible," began Krypton Kate. "Fusing a noble gas like me and a post-transition metal like Bismuth Beth together is akin to fusing two people together. You can't just 'merge' two people. That's like asking us to give up our own individual identities. We will *never* let you do it— and that's why your past fifty experiments have failed."

Of course, if you've ever found out something that you had believed your whole life was false, you would have two opposing thoughts in your brain, just like R.T. did now: on the one hand, it felt like her world was crashing down on her because if she couldn't fuse two atoms together, she couldn't produce new elements. On the other hand, she had just made an astonishing discovery: that atoms were alive and had their own personalities. R.T.'s logical brain flipped back and forth between these two realizations as she reflected on what to do next.

"My belief has been that fusing atoms to make new elements could benefit the world," said R.T. "Imagine an element that has the strength of two atoms inside it. I'm trying to fuse the two of you because Bismuth has high tensile strength and thermal conductivity, and Krypton is plentiful on Earth and is used as a light and energy source. The combination of the two of you could replace the world's reliance on fossil fuels and create a new green energy source."

Bismuth Beth and Krypton Kate looked at each other, eyebrows raised. "We hadn't thought about fusion like *that* before," said Krypton Kate. "We've been focused on existing in our natural state, with the knowledge that fusion would make us vanish."

"The concept of fusion making us stronger is intriguing," said Bismuth Beth. "So would that mean that *all* of our identities and personalities together would exist in this new element?"

"Not exactly," said R.T., uncertain about how to explain the situation. "I believe the strongest traits of each of your personalities would be retained in the new element, and the weaker traits would be eliminated."

"But what are our strongest and weakest traits?" Bismuth Beth asked.

"Let's see," said R.T. "Bismuth Beth, you would still be able to resist being damaged but be unable to heal. And, Krypton Kate, you would keep your usefulness in lighting and energy, but you would have to give up your insulation abilities."

"I still don't understand!" said Bismuth Beth. "What happens to the part of me that doesn't get merged?"

R.T. debated what to say next. Telling the truth would probably petrify the atoms, but she didn't want to lie to them either.

"Well ... those weaker parts of you would disappear forever, and a new element called Ununennium would form," said R.T.

"Would we even *recognize* ourselves anymore?" asked Krypton Kate.

"Well ... uh ..." R.T. tried to find a way to explain. "In human terms, a child has both the DNA imprint of their mother and their father. The most dominant traits are present in the child and not the weaker traits. But the child has their own unique identity and personality."

"So does that mean that Ununennium would have her own personality—and we'd both be *gone*?" asked Krypton Kate.

R.T. nodded slowly and silently.

"Wait a minute," started Bismuth Beth. "Let me get this straight. You want us—to merge together—and give up our personality traits—all because *you* think you can fuse two atoms with your cyclotron and immediately get a new energy source? *And* you've *never* done it before?" Bismuth Beth jabbed a finger in R.T.'s direction.

R.T. wanted to say that the experiment would be a massive breakthrough for science and a once-in-a-generation opportunity, and that the pursuit of science was worth any sacrifice required. But then she remembered something that her grandmother had taught her. *Start from their brain, not yours.*

R.T. always struggled to feel for others because she had

trouble putting herself in their heads. Her grandmother had constantly told R.T. that was her Achilles' heel. Her grandmother wanted to make sure R.T. didn't just succeed in science but in interacting with people as well.

With that insight in mind, R.T. finally spoke. "I understand what you're saying. I'm asking you both to make a huge sacrifice, and it's scary, and it'll completely change your existence. But I'm asking you anyway because global-warming emissions keep increasing year after year. You two could be the heroes that save us all. Isn't that worth the risk?"

"Well, R.T.," said Bismuth Beth, "if you were to merge with another human, would you want to give up your life forever?"

"Me?" R.T. asked, taken aback by the question. "I—I don't think I've found another human who I would want to mind-meld with, other than my grandmother. We shared a lot of the same interests."

"Well, what if we were to put *you* and your grandmother in the cyclotron and fuse you? Let's see how that works out. *Hmm*?" said Bismuth Beth.

"Don't you remember?" Krypton Kate whispered. "She just told us that her grandmother passed away."

Tap-tap-tap. R.T. and the two atoms heard sounds above them. But from where, exactly?

"What is that?" said Krypton Kate. "Did the cyclotron start already? Are we going to get sucked in?"

Stepping back in surprise, R.T. noticed Bismuth Beth looking around to locate the source of the sound. *Tappa-tippy-tap.*

"What is that noise?" asked R.T.

"I think our families are trying to get our attention," said Bismuth Beth.

R.T. looked more closely. The Bismuth and Krypton families were banging their fists on the glass panes of their cubicle, like a carpenter hammering.

"We have to talk to them and get back up there!" shouted Krypton Kate. "They've *never* revealed themselves like this before!"

"But how will we get up to the periodic table?" said Bismuth Beth.

"Do you want me to lift you up?" asked R.T., stretching out her palm.

The two atoms hopped onto R.T.'s palm. R.T. walked them to the periodic table and lifted them to the level of the Bismuths' cubicle.

Bismuth Beth pressed her hands against the glass pane, her nose smushed as she peered inside. She could see her father, Bismuth Barry, her younger brother, Bismuth Ben, her aunt, Bismuth Bertha, and her cousin, Bismuth Brooklyn. But right at the front stood someone who wasn't even in her family—Hydrogen, the oldest atom in the periodic table. He had a golden halo over the large number one on top of him. The other atoms viewed him as their leader.

"Greetings, child," Hydrogen said, loudly and clearly.

"H—Hydrogen?" said Bismuth Beth in shock. She saw consternation on the faces of her family.

Hydrogen wore a stern expression on his face. "Child, you have broken every rule that we have created to protect us. You have placed all of us at risk, and you have changed the course of our existence forever."

Bismuth was wide-eyed and speechless. "Uh, I, um … only did this because—R.T. is planning to fuse me with Krypton Kate and I don't want to lose my personality, so—I was trying to get R.T. to stop this experiment by making her notice me!"

"You have no choice now but to walk down this path and fuse," replied Hydrogen. "In order to have control over fusion, we need to establish an agreement that scientists will have to ask atoms if they want to be fused. Otherwise, millions of us atoms will disappear as more and more scientists experiment with fusion. You have to continue what you started so that our future is secure."

Bismuth Beth, her head lowered, appeared to be accepting the inevitability of her fate. "Dad, Ben, Auntie, Brooklyn, I love you. I hope you'll always remember me and forgive me. And I hope I make you proud by making this new green-energy source." Her eyes welled with tears as she took one final look at her family and Hydrogen.

Krypton Kate grasped Bismuth Beth's hand. "And Hydrogen, thank you for guiding us all—and me. Goodbye."

R.T. lowered her palm and carried Bismuth Beth and Krypton Kate back to the cyclotron's entrance.

"Are you okay?" R.T. asked the atoms gently.

This was one of the rare times that R.T. actually *made* eye contact with whom she was speaking, other than her grandmother.

"I already miss my family," said Bismuth Beth.

"Me, too," lamented Krypton Kate.

"I'm scared of merging, but we have no choice," said Bismuth Beth.

"It'll be a painless fusion," replied R.T. "I promise."

Bismuth Beth and Krypton Kate held each other's hands tightly.

The Fusion Plan ...

R.T. was eager to start the fusion now that she had gotten Bismuth Beth and Krypton Kate's support. Though she had adjusted the two large D-shaped magnets to the maximum amount of force possible earlier that morning, she had just promised Bismuth Beth and Krypton Kate that the fusion would be painless. R.T. quickly reduced the force so the two atoms would be comfortable during this process.

"Okay, Bismuth Beth," began R.T. "You are going to be the target since your atomic number is larger, so you'll move to the back of the cyclotron." R.T. pointed to the far wall of the cyclotron opposite where the atoms stood. "And Krypton Kate, you will be the beam. The magnets will propel you toward Bismuth Beth, and as your speed accelerates, you will hit Bismuth Beth. That fusion will result in the birth of element 119."

"But I thought you said this was going to be painless!" said Krypton Kate. "I would never hit Bismuth Beth like that!"

"No, no, no, it's all going to be okay. Trust me. I've adjusted the force so you will feel like you are seamlessly merging into each other," said R.T. "That being said, I do suggest you both close your eyes because the fusion produces a bright light."

"This is the worst idea ever," Bismuth Beth said as R.T. moved her to the other end of the cyclotron.

Bismuth Beth gave one last wave to Krypton Kate.

At the opposite end, Krypton Kate was pacing anxiously.

R.T. tried to reassure her. "Remember what Hydrogen said. You're both doing this for the rest of the atoms." R.T. pointed toward the periodic table dashboard, where the Krypton family peered into the glass pane at their relative in the cyclotron. "Think about it this way, Krypton Kate. You and Bismuth Beth are going to create a new energy source that can change the entire world. Your family is counting on you."

R.T. watched as Krypton Kate took deep breaths to calm herself, and then finally blurted out the words, "I'm ready."

The Fusion Begins ...

Green arches surrounded Krypton Kate as she gradually approached the two large D-shaped magnets. The entrance doors were closed behind her. She could hear R.T. pressing buttons on the cyclotron's control panel to start up the magnets. Krypton Kate gazed at the vast, blue, circular space between the magnets.

VRRRRRR ... The magnets started to vibrate around her, gradually picking up speed. Krypton Kate shook as she felt herself levitating off the ground, then floating, then soaring. Everything seemed like a blur as Krypton Kate kept accelerating in circles until she reached the speed of light. She flipped around in all sorts of weird positions and was no match for the cyclotron's strong magnetic pull. She tried to grab hold of something—anything—to prevent herself from flying away, but the force was too strong.

"No, no, no—*AHHHHHH!*" Krypton Kate was moving so fast that she couldn't even breathe properly. The blur had been blue at the start of the fusion, but now all she could see was a bunch of green flashes. Suddenly, she saw Bismuth Beth's rainbow-colored hair in front of her.

It happened.

A bright explosion filled the cyclotron. Bismuth Beth and Krypton Kate were no more.

Ununennium was born.

R.T. watched the light gradually fade inside the cyclotron. And this is what she saw ...

Ununennium opened one eye, then the next, blinking rapidly.

"Did it work? Have I really done it?" said R.T., opening the back doors of the cyclotron. Inside, she saw a small white figure with the number 119 on top of its head.

"Ununennium!" R.T. whispered.

"Yes, I am Ununennium," the figure said. "Who are you?"

"I—I can't believe you're here," R.T. said, stunned. "I—am the scientist who created you."

"Are you my mother?"

R.T. blushed as she rushed to explain. "Uh, no, you came from two atoms, Bismuth Beth and Krypton Kate."

"So where are they?"

"They're inside you."

"Inside me?" Ununennium looked down at her body, confused.

"They fused together so that you could be born. I have such big plans for you!"

"What plans? Who are you again?"

Amazed by the triumphant results of this trial, R.T. stretched her open palm toward her newly created atom. Ununennium struggled to get up, wobbling her arms and legs like a baby attempting to take her first steps. Trying to maintain her balance, Ununennium clambered onto R.T.'s palm.

"I have so much to show you," said R.T.

R.T. walked Ununennium over to the periodic table dashboard so that all 118 elements could see the newest addition to their community. Ununennium gazed in wonder at the cubicles in front of her. The Bismuths and Kryptons stared at the new arrival, perhaps uncertain as to whether to mourn their lost family members or cheer for the newly fused element.

Ununennium stood up and said, "I am Ununennium, Element 119."

"Welcome, child," said Hydrogen. "We have high hopes for you. Many of the Bismuths and Kryptons have sacrificed themselves so you could enter the world."

Ununennium absorbed this information and nodded her head.

"Welcome to the world, Ununennium," R.T. said gently, waving at the atoms in the periodic table dashboard. R.T. then walked over to the picture of her grandmother on the wall.

"Ununennium, this is my grandmother, Benny Fishul. She was a famous physicist and my favorite person in the whole world. If only she were here right now! She would have been excited to meet you."

R.T. looked straight into her grandmother's eyes. "Grandma, I did it! I followed the science where it led. I created a new element, and I discovered that all elements are living." R.T. stroked Ununennium's hair with the tip of her finger. "Grandma, looks like you've become a great-grandmother now."

Ununennium smiled at the picture. "Pleased to meet you."

R.T. walked over to her desk, grabbed a glass cube structure, and attached it to the periodic table dashboard right beneath the Francium cubicle. This would be Ununennium's new home—119.

Ununennium let out a delicate yawn and curled up on R.T.'s palm.

"Why don't you rest? You must be exhausted from the fusion process," said R.T. She gently put Ununennium to sleep on her goggles.

As Ununennium slept, R.T. turned to her journal. *Click. Flip.* She began writing on a new page:

5. Test/ Experiment:
During this fifty-first trial, I was able to fuse bismuth and krypton to make element 119. It should have the ability to resist damage (like bismuth) and also have the ability to produce energy (like krypton).

6. Analysis:
Since I have now discovered atoms are alive, and each element has its own identity, I can only fuse them together if they give their permission. Just because I want to do another trial doesn't mean they will allow me to do so.

7. Conclusion:
Therefore, fusing ten new elements (including element 119) is possible—as long as I get support from the atoms.

R.T. sighed in satisfaction, proud of her success.

In one day, R.T. grew as a scientist and a new element entered our world. Amazing, isn't it?

R.T., without even knowing it, had been dedicating all her time to living things. And the atoms, well, their big reveal would change the course of chemistry forever. And it was all thanks to Bismuth Beth and Krypton Kate, who found courage in fear. As for Ununennium, her story is yet to be told. She's part Bismuth Beth, and part Krypton Kate—and all Ununennium, Element 119.

HOW ARE NEW ELEMENTS NAMED?

Lawrencium. Moscovium. Dubnium. Oganesson. These element names might sound weird. Where did they come from? How *did* these elements get their names?

The IUPAC (International Union of Pure and Applied Chemistry) has many rules about how to name an element. The rules say that an element can be named after a mythological character or concept (like thorium for Thor), a mineral (such as gadolinium for gadolinite), a place (for example, francium for France), a property of the element (like radium for its radioactivity), or a scientist (like einsteinium for Albert Einstein.)

Elements near the end of the periodic table that have an atomic number greater than 100 used to have a name related to their atomic number. For instance, the 118th element used to be called "ununoctium" because it loosely translates to "one-one-eight" in Latin. When it was called that, the chemical symbol was Uuo.

But once the IUPAC approves the element's

name, the chemical symbol switches to two letters. Nowadays, element 118 is called oganesson, named for the scientist Yuri Oganessian, with the chemical symbol Og.

Element 119 has not been discovered yet. For now, we call it ununennium, or "one-one-nine" in Latin, with the chemical symbol Uue. But if a scientist manages to produce this element and proposes to the IUPAC a new name, its chemical symbol will change.

So, now that you know the rules, what would *you* call element 119?

ELEMENTOPHOBIA

I don't use lithium batteries,
Or drink from aluminum cans.
I avoid sodium salt shakers
And iron frying pans.

I disapprove of bananas—
The potassium makes me shiver.
When someone mentions oxygen,
My lips can't help but quiver.

I cringe at radium watches,
And I don't like gold at all.
The sight of a rhenium jet engine
Sends me straight up the wall.

I just despise thermometers—
There's mercury inside.
I shriek when I see nitrogen,
And argon makes me hide.

At the slightest hint of chlorine,
I don't seem to feel my best.
Turns out, I got these fears after
I *flunked* the chemistry test!

MEET THE NOBLE GAS FAMILY

(My Imagination. Totally Not Real.)

Helium: Helium is the youngest member of the family, which explains his high-pitched voice. By the way, *you* can get a high-pitched voice when you inhale helium from a party balloon! Helium is longing for a friend, but because he is a noble gas, he can't bond. Helium is one of the lightest elements in the periodic table, so he can fly. Also, he can emit a bright pink light when activated by heat.

Neon: Neon is Helium's older brother, and so he has one more shell and more electrons. Unlike Helium, Neon is more of a traditional noble gas—laid-back and quiet. Neon can often be found meditating, reading, or riding through the coaster he built, reminiscent of tubes in a neon sign.

18

Argon: Argon is Helium's cousin whose favorite pastime fits her name perfectly. Argon's name means "inactive," which is appropriate because she is often sleeping.

36

Krypton: Krypton is Helium's mother who, like Helium, also has a special talent: she can shoot green lasers from her fingertips. She doesn't understand Helium's efforts to bond, but she does appreciate photography lighting—and keeps it lit!

54

Xenon: Xenon is Helium's loving father who helps Helium realize he isn't the only one who's different in his family. Just like his wife (Krypton), Xenon has a passion for photography and always carries around his camera.

Radon: Radon is Helium's radioactive aunt. (Ooh, never thought I'd write the words "radioactive" and "aunt" together in a sentence.) But Radon can be helpful, too, as she works at the hospital as an X-ray technician.

Oganesson: Oganesson is Helium's radioactive grandfather. (Two more words that I never thought I'd write together!) See the number on his cane? That number, 118, is his atomic number. He's the oldest, so he has the most electrons and shells. Oganesson likes to tell stories to his youngest grandson. But whenever Oganesson gets angry, his radiation glows bright green.

OPERATION BOND

(A Helium Story)

Helium leaned against a wall of the chemistry school building, watching the other atom children play on the orange playground equipment. They were sharing their electrons with each other and playing games. Some atom children shared two electrons, others four, and others six in order to bond with each other. Then they would bounce around and play happily, swirling and twirling in the air above the playground. Two atom children, Hydrogen and Carbon, sat together on the swings talking to each other.

Carbon said to Hydrogen, "Watch this! I can swing super high!"

Hydrogen boasted, "I bet I can swing higher than you! Let's race!"

Helium thought their competition looked fun—so much so that he wished he had someone to race against. He looked over at the merry-go-round and saw another atom child, Phosphorus, and her two friends, Sodium and Potassium, playing tag. Sodium was "it," and as Phosphorus accelerated her pace, her body and hair changed color from orange to red to purple. Helium marveled at the sight and thought that Phosphorus would make a great friend.

As Phosphorus and Sodium chased each other in circles, Helium could hear Phosphorus taunting Sodium, "You can't catch me, 'cause I'm on fire!"

Just as she said these words, Phosphorus' excitement made both her hair and electrons burst into flame.

Helium was shocked to see Phosphorus ignite herself, and he longed for an atom child with a superpower to be a friend of his own.

In the past, Helium had tried and tried to bond with other atoms, but he could not. Helium came from the noble gas family and had a very special attribute. Helium had two electrons in his outer shell, making him perfectly stable. He and all the members of his family had no need to exchange electrons with other atoms. So whenever another atom child tried to bond with Helium to play together, that atom sharply bounced off of Helium's outer shell. Helium was always left alone, feeling sad and friendless.

Helium went home that day, eager to share potential recess friendships with his family. His electrons ricocheted around his shell as he dashed into the living room. His brother, Neon, was meditating beside the bookcase as Helium approached.

"Hey, Neon, guess what? I think I found some atoms on the playground that I'd like to be friends with," Helium squeaked.

"*Meh*, that isn't going to work," Neon responded in a monotone voice that was lower than Helium's. "Remember, noble gases can't bond."

"Your brother is right," added Krypton, Helium's mother, who was sitting on the couch while pointing lasers from her fingertips at the walls. "You're already stable, so you don't need to have friends."

His mother's words depressed Helium. He wanted a friend so badly, even though he was a noble gas. A friend would be someone he could talk to, share experiences with, and even complain to about his family members. Helium sulked as he drifted through the hallway. He passed by pictures his father, Xenon, had taken with

his camera. There was one of Helium's cousin, Argon, one of Aunt Radon, and even one depicting the whole family.

Helium stopped at his grandfather, Oganesson's, room. Helium glided in and said, "Grandpa, there were some atoms on the playground today that I want to be my friends. I know I'm a noble gas, but could I *still* be friends with them?"

"Why, that's a HORRIBLE idea! You can't be friends with other atoms!" Oganesson roared, his radiation glowing brighter than ever, so strong that he could zap anything in his path. His white hair stood on end, and his electrons spun.

"But you don't know what I mean!" cried Helium. "The other atoms are always racing each other and showing off their cool superpowers, but *I* don't have someone to play with!" Helium's despair made his voice sound higher in pitch, and his electron shell tilted at an unusual 45-degree angle.

"Listen to me, Helium. When I was younger, I tried making friends on the playground, too, but my radiation hurt the others because my powers were hard to control. Even worse, I repelled the other atoms! I'm just trying to save you from the same disappointment."

"I appreciate that, Grandpa." Helium softened his tone as he realized his grandfather's sharp reaction came from a place of love. "But I have to try for myself."

As Helium slowly exited the room, he pondered his family's reactions and realized how similar his experience was to his grandfather's. Should he try to make friends and risk the same failure as his grandfather? Should he just not try at all? Could his experience be *different* from that of his grandfather?

Helium's reflections continued during the next day at school. Helium floated to his blue desk near the back of his classroom. Each desk had the students' element square on it. Helium stared at the poster of the periodic table on the wall, which doubled as the attendance list each day. He silently wished that his teacher wouldn't go into the bonding unit today after finishing the chemical reaction unit. Helium disliked being taught how to do something he structurally couldn't do.

As Helium settled at his desk, he heard whispers from his classmates about how he wasn't able to bond with them on the playground yesterday. He pretended not to hear their words, even though they made him feel embarrassed. His electron shells began to tilt, heating his body until it began to slowly expand. This only made Helium feel more mortified. He tried to slow down his breathing, exhaling with long breaths to expel the maximum gas possible. Just then, the lesson started.

"Okay, class, today's lesson is about the different types of *bonding*!" rang the voice of Helium's teacher, Ms. Rubidium.[4]

Oh, no, not the B-word, thought Helium.

Ms. Rubidium said, "First up, ionic bonding! This is the type of bond in which one atom will give one electron to the other. One will have a positive charge and the other negative. They always say 'opposites attract'!" The class laughed at that line. "Let's all get up from our desks and try to do this with a partner!"

"Okay, I'll try," mumbled Helium to himself. "I only have two electrons, so nothing will go wrong—I hope."

---

[4] To learn how and why atoms bond, see page 115.

Helium cautiously walked toward Cobalt, who hadn't found a partner yet.

"Uh, hey . . . can I bond with you?" Helium asked nervously, in a higher voice than before.

"Uh, I'm not sure about th—" Cobalt started. Before Cobalt could even finish her sentence, Helium inadvertently repelled her, sending her sailing across the room.

"I'll find another partner!" Cobalt hurriedly yelled from afar as she regained her bearings.

Helium's classmates kept avoiding him throughout the rest of the group work on covalent bonds and polar bonds. "He really doesn't bond with other atoms! He must be very selfish!" whispered one atom student to another.

Helium continued to ignore their comments as he moped alone in the back of the room. He thought again about his grandfather's words. Helium resolved to rebel and give bonding another try—at lunchtime.

———

As Helium glided to the cafeteria entrance, he gazed at the periodic table-shaped lunch tables. He filled his tray with molecular macaroni and periodic pizza, and then surveyed the cafeteria for a less-crowded table. He spotted Hydrogen and Lithium sitting together. Helium considered that his bonding chances might be greater if he sat between Hydrogen and Lithium, whose atomic numbers were one and three, respectively. Helium was second in the periodic table, so perhaps following the natural order of the periodic table would help him to bond.

Eager to test his hypothesis, Helium rushed over to the gap between Hydrogen and Lithium. "Hey, can I join you?" Helium asked Hydrogen.

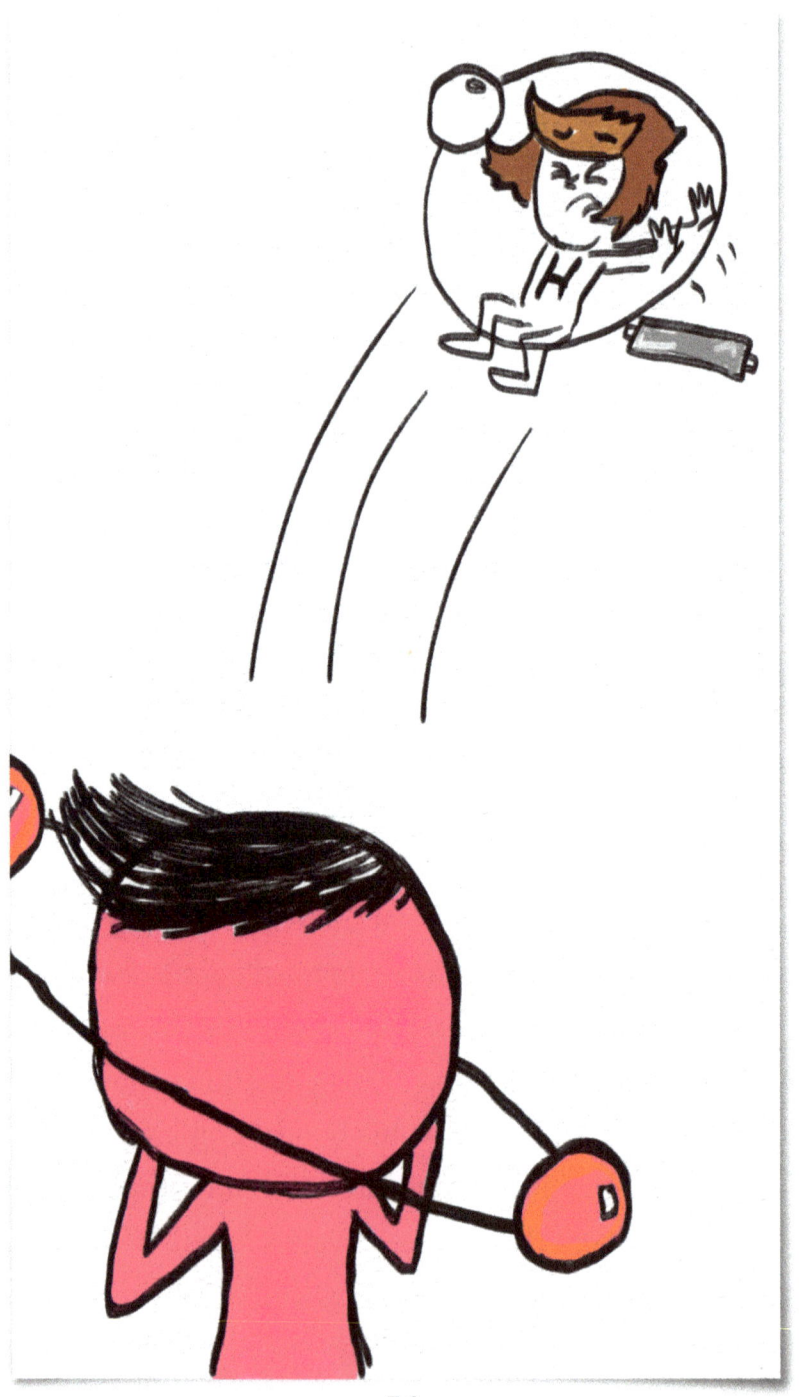

Hydrogen stared at him warily. Suddenly, Helium could feel it happening—again. Hydrogen slammed against the wall, repelled by Helium's force. The force was so strong that Hydrogen's lunch flew off its tray and splattered onto the floor, making a huge mess!

"I'm so sorry," Helium apologized, feeling deeply embarrassed and humiliated.

All of his classmates heard the crash and eyed Helium with disdain. Helium escaped the cafeteria in distress.

"How will a noble gas like me ever make a friend?" muttered Helium to himself.

As Helium looked up at a nearby bulletin board, he noticed posters for a school open house to be held that night. An opportunity?

"Looks like I've got myself one last attempt," he said aloud. But he didn't feel very hopeful.

A few hours after school ended, Helium's family got into their ellipse-shaped car and buckled their seatbelts. Xenon was at the wheel.

"Helium, how did your bonding attempts go today?" whispered Oganesson.

"Not so well." Helium sighed. "I don't think I'll ever be able to make a friend. You and the family were right. I'm just a nonbonding noble gas nobody." As Helium stared out the window, he considered giving up on his idea to make friends. Lost in the bubble of his thoughts, he worried about repelling someone if he tried to make friends at the open house. Perhaps he should heed the words of his family from now on and give up.

The car came to a stop beside the school building, and the

family slowly exited, Helium being last. There were other atom families waiting to go inside the school, but Helium and his family stood at a distance.

I can't bond, but maybe I could offer to help prepare the decorations, thought Helium.

He moved toward his teacher. "Um, Ms. Rubidium, earlier I noticed the balloons that needed to be set up in the cafeteria. Could I please help blow some of them up? I'm good at blowing up balloons at parties."

"Of course you can, Helium!" Ms. Rubidium looked at her watch. "It's 8:25 right now, and the doors won't open until 8:35. You can enter the cafeteria using that door over there," said Ms. Rubidium, pointing.

"Okay!" replied Helium. He went inside and worked quickly, until he had only a few balloons left to blow up. As he inhaled and exhaled, filling a long yellow balloon, he noticed a small white figure whooshing in the air outside. Helium realized it was Hydrogen, showing off her flying abilities.

"*Woo-hoo!* I'm the lightest element!" Hydrogen exclaimed.

She zipped around a tree and spun again as she landed on the sidewalk. The atom families applauded.

Wait a minute, thought Helium. *I can fly, too.*

Helium was the second-lightest element in the entire periodic table, which gave him the power to fly higher than most of the other atom children.

"Could flying help me to bond?" Helium wondered aloud.

He continued to ponder this question as he blew up the remaining balloons.

Minutes later, the school doors opened, welcoming everyone inside. The cafeteria was filled with long tables around the perimeter for students to display their work and show how each one was special in some way.

Helium noticed a sign beside the cafeteria exit door, with a red arrow pointing outside.

I wonder what's happening outside the building, thought Helium.

And with that, he snuck out of the building, leaving his family inside the cafeteria.

More tables lined the wall next to the playground. Just then, Helium noticed another familiar atom from recess. Phosphorus!

"Check this out, everyone!" Phosphorus shouted.

Suddenly, her body color transitioned from her regular orange to a vivid, eerie, green glow. When the other atom children outside saw her radiant light, they walked over and gazed in wonder.

One atom child joked, "Who needs a flashlight when we have Phosphorus!"

Everyone laughed.

"I can glow in the dark, too," whispered Helium to himself. "But how can *that* help me bond?"

Then Helium realized something. He had been focusing so hard on how to make himself like all the other atom children that he hadn't spent time thinking about what made him special.

"If only I could combine my two talents in a way that would help me to bond, without repelling anyone," Helium said to himself.

He could fly higher than most atom children and glow bright

pink when activated by heat . . . and just like that, an idea popped into Helium's head. Operation Bond was born!

─────────────────

Helium made his way toward a wall near the crowd. Then he floated to an elevation where everyone could see him, about three-quarters up the wall's height. He positioned himself close to the school's heating vent, until he could feel his electrons heat up. The resulting reaction made a vivid pink glow burst out of Helium. He felt like a rocket loaded with light inside him, about to launch. The pink glow grew beyond Helium's body, almost like an iridescent halo that bathed the entire playground and blacktop.

Helium heard the crowd murmuring ...

"Where's that light coming from?"

"It's so beautiful!"

"I love this color!"

Helium began to glow even brighter! Soon, one atom child noticed that Helium was the light source and ran below him. Another atom child started bopping in the light, which led to others bopping and bonding with each other. Just like during recess, some atom children were sharing two electrons, some four, and others six. Some of the atoms looked up at Helium and waved! Helium waved back while he concentrated on producing the light.

The atom children bonded and danced as if they were at a disco party, exchanging their electrons. Helium felt like he was the party's disco ball, making his light shine even brighter. Thousands of hot-pink pulses of light shot all over the school like lasers, bouncing off the walls and windows.

But Helium wasn't finished. He prepared for his big finale.

Helium combined all the laser lights to form a single giant ray. The atom children followed the ray's direction, while Helium bent his body back to make the ray go through the cafeteria window. Everyone waited to see what would happen next.

Inside the cafeteria, the bright pink ray of light bathed everyone's eyes. Through the big windows Helium could see all the atoms, including his family, staring at the ray in surprise.

Helium began rotating rapidly, making the ray revolve around the room. The balloons were drawn to the ray like a magnet, clustering together and flying out an open cafeteria window.

"*Ahh!* What's happening? Is there a balloon bandit?" Ms. Rubidium shrieked.

Helium felt a tingling sensation as everyone looked up to see him hovering twenty feet in the air. Helium could see Ms. Rubidium running away to hide in the kitchen. Helium didn't take this personally because rubidium is a highly reactive element that panics quickly.

The balloons floated out the cafeteria window in all directions. The atom children squealed in delight and ran to the blacktop to catch them.

Once again, Helium heard words that delighted him.

"Do you change color?"

"Can you glow *brighter*?"

"I want to see the lasers again!"

"*Whoa-whoa-whoa!*" Helium laughed. "Take it easy, everyone!"

Just then, Helium saw his mother and Neon standing outside the school. Helium felt anxious, wondering how they would react to his attempt at bonding. Would they be mad at what he was doing?

But Helium couldn't stop now. He could feel himself glowing even brighter. He was sure that his electrons could be seen clearly by everyone now.

Next outside was Xenon, Helium's dad. He stared at Helium in amazement. Atom children surrounded Xenon, cheering for Helium. Xenon looked ... proud?

Helium watched as Xenon took out his beloved camera and pointed it his way.

"This is truly a special moment, Helium!" Xenon yelled. "I'll take pictures so we'll remember it!"

Tears of joy formed in Helium's eyes. His family had gathered for *him*. They were cheering along with the crowd.

Helium beamed at everyone, thrilled that Operation Bond had worked. As the atom children cheered and applauded, he gradually floated downward, his bright pink light slowly fading to his body's original color.

"Whew!" said Helium, still buzzing from the experience. He immediately ran to his father and wrapped his arms around him.

"So," said Xenon. "You were trying to bond, weren't you, Helium?"

Helium's electrons vibrated as he worried if his dad was upset.

"I—I was," Helium stuttered.

Then he noticed his mother. She wasn't scowling, like he expected. She was, instead, smiling brightly. Neon and Radon both grinned.

Just then, Fluorine and Oxygen from Helium's class came running toward Helium.

"Helium!" Oxygen shouted. "I LOVED that pink color! How did you do it?"

"And seeing the lasers combine into a giant pink ray that freed all the balloons from the cafeteria was so awesome!" Fluorine joined in. "We all had fun!"

"And it makes me feel as if I just bonded with *you*, Helium," Oxygen chimed in.

Helium saw Phosphorus and Potassium floating toward him.

The exciting display that Helium had created earlier made both atom children burst into flame—one bluish-green and the other lilac purple.

"Helium," Phosphorus started. "That—was—the most AMAZING thing I've EVER seen! I never knew you could *do* that! Especially the part with the cool lasers and letting all the balloons out!"

"You really brightened up the ENTIRE open house, Helium! The balloons were so fun!" Potassium exclaimed.

"Thanks to all of you," Helium responded, realizing he had found a way to befriend his classmates.

"Helium, it's time to go," his mother said. "You must be tired after all that."

"Bye, everyone! See you tomorrow!" Helium shouted from a distance, waving as he and his family floated back to the car and headed home.

"I can't believe that I was finally able to bond," Helium said out loud in his bedroom. As Helium got ready for bed, he remembered what a great night they had all experienced. "Maybe I *can* be different from my family after all."

Helium's father entered the room, smiling. "You know," Xenon whispered, leaning toward Helium. "I've been keeping something a secret for a long time because I didn't want anyone to think I was weird compared to the rest of the family but—I actually bonded with Fluorine and Oxygen in my class when I was at school."

"Did you really? I thought *I* was the only one who wanted to bond!" replied Helium. "How did you do it?"

"I was born with a larger atomic radius than the rest of the family," explained Xenon. "This means my ionization energy is minimal to the electrons and I can bond, unlike other noble gases."

Xenon turned to the wall and put up a photo. Helium realized it was a photo that his father had taken of him at the open house when Helium was busy making the pink light.

Then Xenon turned and embraced Helium tightly. "Your mom and I are so proud of you."

Helium had never felt more loved and accepted than in that moment.

As Helium rested his head on his pillow at bedtime, he smiled happily. "Looks like there's more than one way to bond after all."

WHAT ARE NOBLE GASES?
(The Facts. Period.)

The noble gases are elements located in group 18 of the periodic table. They are colorless, odorless, and inert, which means that they keep to themselves and don't react or bond with most elements. Bonding is basically two atoms exchanging electrons with each other to become stable. But noble gases are already stable, which makes them unique in the periodic table. So they rarely bond with other atoms.

Also, most noble gases can glow a bright color when activated by heat, which is really cool to watch!

The seven noble gases are helium, neon, argon, krypton, xenon, radon, and oganesson. Let me introduce you to them one by one, in the order they appear in the periodic table:

Helium: A noble gas with the chemical symbol He and atomic number 2. It glows hot pink, and its name comes from the Greek word *helios*, which means "sun." Helium is used for blimps, rocket fuel, and its most popular use—party balloons!

Neon: A noble gas with the chemical symbol Ne and atomic number 10. It glows reddish-orange. If you've ever driven through a busy city at night and seen glowing signs on the buildings, then you're pretty familiar with this element. Plus, neon can also be used in lasers! Pretty cool, huh?

Argon: A noble gas with the chemical symbol Ar and atomic number 18. It glows purple, and its name comes from the Greek word *argos*, meaning "inactive." Makes sense, since argon is an inert gas! You can find argon in light bulbs.

Krypton: A noble gas with the chemical symbol Kr and atomic number 36. It glows bluish-green and is one of the few noble gases that can bond with at least one other element. You heard me right—krypton *can* bond with fluorine! As for its uses, krypton is used in lights, lasers, and photographic flashbulbs.

Xenon: A noble gas with the chemical symbol Xe and atomic number 54. It glows blue and is another noble gas that can bond. Because xenon atoms are wider than other noble gases, xenon can bond with both fluorine *and* oxygen! Xenon can be found in flashbulbs in cameras and also in Mars' atmosphere! Isn't *that* out of this world?

Radon: A radioactive noble gas with the chemical symbol Rn and atomic number 86. Solid radon glows yellow, but its light turns red when it cools. Although you may consider radon helpful when you learn how it's used in X-rays, its radiation can also cause lung cancer.

Oganesson: A radioactive noble gas with the chemical symbol Og and atomic number 118. This is the last and heaviest element on the periodic table and was named after the scientist Yuri Oganessian. Oganesson doesn't exist naturally on Earth—scientists have to make it in a lab. So far, only a few atoms of this element have ever been produced.

THE RADIUM

It asked me, "Do you like eights?"
Then I responded, "Eights are great!"
It said, "Well, what about eighty-eights?"
"Eighty-eights are twice as great!"

No matter what, every eighty-eight'd
Be sure to make me twice as elated,
And then I'll jump and cheer with glee,
Except for what it then said to me—

"Well, if you like eights, my eighty-eight'd
Been outnumbered, underestimated—
I am the 88-proton Radium
Stuck in this glass tube from the Marie Curie Stadium."

There was a small label on the tube that read,
"Do not open, or else you'll be dead."
The Radium screamed, "Let me out of here, kid!"
As I tried my best not to open the lid.

But that atomic number, I was tempted by it—
I wouldn't mind if I opened it just a *little* bit.
The Radium released in a poisonous haze
And I felt as if I was lost in a maze.

My eyes felt heavy, and due to that Radium,
My lungs stopped breathing and my bones decayed-ium.
I've never been exposed to radiation before—
I don't think I should like eights anymore.

WHAT IS RADIUM?

Radium is an element in the alkaline earth metal family with the chemical symbol Ra and atomic number—well, it's pretty obvious if you've read my poem, "*The Radium*." Spoiler alert: it's 88.

Radium was discovered by the Polish chemist Marie Curie. While in her lab in France, she tried to separate substances from a rock called pitchblende and ended up finding something glowing inside— actually, two somethings! She had discovered two new elements that she would name polonium (after her home country of Poland) and radium. These elements emitted bright, eerie rays of green light that Marie Curie called "radiation." Yes, she did invent that word.

Soon enough, word spread of Madame Curie's discovery. Everyone started to use radium to make their watches, lipstick, and even water glow! Actors and dancers put radium on their costumes to make them look like they glowed in the dark. People thought radium was like a magic potion. They were partially right, as radium could treat cancer—but it could make people sick, too. As it turns out, people who used all these radium products were unknowingly being poisoned by them, including Marie Curie herself!

Although weak from the radiation poisoning, Madame Curie and her discovery changed chemistry. She became the first woman to win a—no, TWO Nobel Prizes! She was so famous that a building called the Radium Institute was built in honor of her research. Later, the name was changed to the Curie Institute. Marie Curie eventually died of radium poisoning at the age of 66. It is said that all of her books remain radioactive.

Nowadays, people have stopped using radium for products such as watches and makeup. But radium is still used for cancer-treating medication.

Marie Curie (1867-1934) did groundbreaking research on how metals can emit rays, and she discovered two elements: polonium and radium.

CHEMISTRY LAND: THE ORIGIN

(All in My Head)

When the very first atoms and elements were born in the bellies of stars, a world was created long before Earth.

A world of wonder and connections. A world where atoms resided. A world called Chemistry Land. That world still exists … in my imagination.

Chemistry Land's many landmarks include the Electron Eatery, where the atoms dine on molecular meatballs, atomic avocado toast, or chemical cannolis. Thorium's Emporium is a popular store where atoms shop. Periodic Park is home to the C.O.N. Gardens— C.O.N. is short for "Carbon-Oxygen-Nitrogen," the three atoms who founded and take care of the garden.

As the atom population of Chemistry Land grew, the bravest ones wanted to explore Earth. These atoms allowed humankind to discover them, which caused all sorts of scientific advancements to be made, like the creation of light bulbs and X-rays. Energized by their ability to influence Earth, these atoms began communicating to their peers in Chemistry Land about the needs and wants of humans.

In Chemistry Land, atoms realized that they could form compounds by bonding with each other. This allowed the atoms to put their bonding to use to produce things for humans. The compounds are made in Chemistry Land and then transported to Earth. For instance, Earth got water when a daring oxygen atom wanted to see what would happen if she bonded with two hydrogen atoms.

All was well until there was a big argument in Chemistry Land. Some atoms felt they were more important than others. For example, Carbon was fighting Oxygen, and Sodium was fighting Iron. They didn't realize that Chemistry Land needed all of them to function.

And then came Dmitri Mendeleev, the father of the periodic table on Earth.

When he invented the first version of the periodic table, the atoms on Earth were shocked at his depiction of all the elements and his organization of the elements in families. The atoms thought this could help resolve the argument in Chemistry Land, so they copied Mendeleev's table.

When the Earth atoms ventured back to Chemistry Land and told the other atoms about Mendeleev, the other atoms realized that there was a lot more in common between them than they initially thought. They then came up with an idea: there should be a common location in Chemistry Land where atoms of different elements could work together. And the building should pay tribute to Mendeleev's table.

Nowadays, in Chemistry Land, the Periodic Table Building stands as its most iconic landmark. The atoms have gotten the hang of using their compounds to produce things for humans. And they've all figured out how to get themselves organized, be useful, and have fun.

Chemistry Land occasionally even invites visitors from Earth who are passionate about chemistry, like one certain girl: Maysa, whose adventure is just about to begin.

(You can read her story starting on page 78.)

SAVING THE ATOMS

(A Fluorine Story)

Maysa stared at her science group mates with discomfort. James poured a full cup of vegetable oil into a glass while Kayla impatiently waited to add the water. Sarah and Liam argued about which food coloring they should add to the mixture—red or blue. Dara struggled to open the Alka-Seltzer packaging, which resulted in one of the tablets being broken in two. Maysa's math and science teacher, Ms. Edwards, had given clear instructions about how to do the science experiment, but the group wasn't following them. The directions were to fill a glass with three-quarters of a cup of vegetable oil and a quarter cup of water, add four to five drops of red food coloring and an Alka-Seltzer tablet, and observe what happens.

Even though Maysa was nine years old, she already knew she wanted to be a chemist when she grew up. She had memorized all 118 elements of the periodic table by the time she was seven years old, along with their chemical symbols, atomic numbers, and uses. Even her t-shirt today had a picture of an atom on it. But Maysa was not loving this class science experiment.

The work process of her group mates was chaotic. Maysa knew exactly how the experiment should be conducted, but what she didn't know was how to get her group back on track. If she

78

told them what to do, they would think she was being bossy. If she said nothing, then the experiment would go awry. So instead, Maysa imagined in her head how the experiment would work if she could do it by herself, mentally distancing herself from the group interaction.

Finally, the dismissal bell rang throughout the school. Relieved, Maysa grabbed her backpack and headed home. As soon as she arrived, she grabbed her chemistry set from a side table in her room.

"I can't wait to build molecules and make atoms bond," she whispered to herself.

Maysa sat down with her legs crossed. She lifted the lid open and carefully took out the magnetic atoms of different sizes and colors, the play mat, and the instruction book. Within five minutes, she had already constructed water, carbon dioxide, methane, sodium chloride, carbon monoxide, and ammonia.

When she was about to attach a hydrogen atom to an oxygen atom to form hydrogen peroxide, two eyes suddenly popped onto the hydrogen atom's surface, along with eyebrows, a nose, and a mouth. Then two arms and two legs sprouted out of the atom, followed by hands and feet.

"Hey, Maysa! I'm Hydrogen," the atom announced. "I'm so glad to see you!"

"What are you?!" shrieked Maysa. Stunned, she flung the atom onto the floor. "How did you get here? What do you want? Are you real?"

"Oh, it takes time for humans to understand atoms like me. Take deep breaths while you listen to what I have to say. I'm here because I need your help to save Chemistry Land. We've scanned all the people of the world for someone who has memorized the entire periodic table, is very creative and can solve problems, and is a girl. You're at the top of our list! Congratulations! Take my hand—we need to go to Chemistry Land right away."

Hydrogen grabbed Maysa's hand and she immediately shrank in size, making the chemistry set loom as large as an elephant.

"What's happening?" cried Maysa in shock.

"Don't worry, this is completely normal. You have to reduce in size before you can enter Chemistry Land," Hydrogen responded.

Maysa walked unsteadily with Hydrogen, adjusting to her new diminutive size. She suddenly spied sparkly pink and blue light spiraling in circles in front of her. The circle kept enlarging, with gold dust popping along its surface.

"This," Hydrogen told Maysa, "is the portal to where I live, Chemistry Land. We must hurry and run through it."

Hydrogen pushed Maysa through the circular portal. Maysa felt her body lighten, almost like a leaf picked up by an autumn breeze. Maysa glanced down at herself and realized she was now an atom.

"Atoms aren't supposed to be alive," she declared.

"Well, *I'm* alive," Hydrogen stated. "Chemistry Land is the place where atoms bond and make chemical reactions so that humans can be supplied with the things they use every day."

Maysa tried to process what Hydrogen had just said. The atoms from her chemistry set were living things in this new world.

"Whoa ... this is so cool!" Maysa's fear was ebbing away, replaced by curiosity and wonder as she gazed at the bustling atomic city beneath the pink-and-golden-orange tinted sky.

The atoms that lived in Chemistry Land were chatting and bonding into molecules with each other. Whenever two or more atoms bonded, a honeysuckle aroma wafted pleasingly through the air, and the atoms made a loud snap. Maysa and Hydrogen passed by atoms twirling and hovering in the air as they reacted.

Transparent buildings shaped like mittens caught Maysa's attention because each finger was curled like an ocean wave. Every building had a white chalk-like outline along its perimeter, like a corpse at a crime scene. Alongside the buildings were bushes and trees that resembled inflatable balloons with assorted chemical element squares sprouting from their tops.

"The biggest building in Chemistry Land," Hydrogen shared with Maysa, "is our workplace, the Periodic Table."

Maysa saw a huge, vertical structure shaped like the periodic table that stretched as far as her eyes could see. It had a silver door in the front.

"What's inside it?" asked Maysa.

"This building is divided into 118 color-coded cubicles, and one atom of each element works in its cubicle every day. There are elevator stations on either side of the building so that the larger mass elements can move up and down periods."

Just as Maysa began getting her bearings, a noxious smell invaded her nostrils.

She wrinkled her nose and asked, "Hydrogen, what is that smell?"

"That's Fluorine! That's why I brought you to Chemistry Land! Fluorine must have accelerated his plans to suck up all the other atoms' electrons!" Hydrogen yelled.

Maysa could hear atoms shriek in fear as the odor of steamed Brussels sprouts filled the air. Fluorine was in his gaseous state with a lime-green cloud swirling around him, making his arms and legs nearly invisible. The predatory cloud lurked over Chemistry Land, greedily waiting to snatch the electrons of any atoms in his path.

"Quick! We'd better hide!" panicked Hydrogen. "WE could be the next atoms whose electrons Fluorine will steal!"

As the two dashed behind the Periodic Table building, Maysa and Hydrogen continued to hear and smell Fluorine sucking up electrons as rapidly as a black hole.

"I'm going to be the MOST POWERFUL, MOST SUPERIOR atom in all of Chemistry Land!" Fluorine announced, followed by a cackle. "You atoms never took me seriously! You thought I could only be used in toothpaste. But I'm *WAY* MORE THAN THAT! I can create nuclear power and produce electricity! I'm going to take control of Chemistry Land and flood it with fluorine atoms until we rule the Periodic Table! All I need now is LOTS of negative energy!"

Fifteen minutes later, Fluorine had crossed nearly every corner of Chemistry Land, sucking up electrons, tinting anything in his path green. Fluorine had now expanded in size such that he was as big as the Periodic Table building.

"I'm so close to being the most powerful atom in all of Chemistry Land!" he growled.

All the victimized atoms who had lost their electrons

whimpered in fear, laying paralyzed on the ground, unable to move or bond.

Meanwhile, Hydrogen and Maysa darted past nearby transparent houses, petrified about becoming Fluorine's next two victims.

"Quick! We need a plan!" Maysa cried. "Look! There's a house over there!"

The two peered inside it, desperately searching for a weapon they could use to fight Fluorine. Maysa's eyes landed on a picture frame inside the house, which had the letters "Ca" on the front. She immediately recognized those letters, because it was the chemical symbol of calcium.

"Calcium can neutralize fluorine, right?" she asked Hydrogen. "Maybe since I'm originally human, I can produce a lot of calcium from my bones to neutralize him!"

"But Fluorine's become so big!" responded Hydrogen. "I don't think you'll be able to produce enough calcium to overwhelm him!"

Maysa strained to emit calcium from her body. No luck. She tried again. No dice. She tried one last time to prove she could produce calcium. Nothing, again.

"You're right, Hydrogen, I can't do it," Maysa said, defeated.

"Let's talk to Calcium and see if he has any ideas," offered Hydrogen, banging on the door and yelling Calcium's name.

The door opened. "Did I hear someone say my name?" asked a turquoise atom that looked twenty times larger than Hydrogen.

"Fluorine is sucking up all the atoms' electrons. Can you produce enough calcium to neutralize him?" asked Hydrogen, breathlessly.

"I can bring together all my calcium brothers and sisters, but that could take hours." Calcium looked out the window and pointed to the massive green cloud. "There's Fluorine coming! I'd better hide!" he shouted.

He ran and slid across the room in a panicked manner, consistent with the behavior of an alkaline earth metal.

"If Calcium can't help us, let's get out of here!" shrieked Maysa, watching Fluorine's looming green cloud nearing. Maysa and Hydrogen slammed the door and bolted away from the house. Seconds later, Fluorine arrived, forcing himself inside Calcium's house. He quickly moved toward the two small feet trying to hide under the teal curtains. Fluorine grabbed them with his gas tentacles. At a distance, Hydrogen and Maysa could witness all of this through the home's transparent wall.

"*Aha*! Those twenty electrons shall be mine," Fluorine declared, hoovering them up like a vacuum.

Calcium's body fell to the floor with a thud.

"Oh no!" cried Maysa.

Then she saw that Fluorine's outer shells were packed with negatively charged electrons. An idea struck her.

"I've got it!" she exclaimed.

"What?" Hydrogen asked, breathlessly.

"We need to make an extra-positive force to stop Fluorine," said Maysa. "But we're going to need another atom with a lot of protons. Then we can knock all of the electrons loose from Fluorine's outer shells."

"Let's give it a try. This situation is desperate!" yelled Hydrogen.

But even though it was her plan, Maysa worried it might not succeed. She preferred working by herself—and had since first grade. Just as in the science experiment at school with her assigned group, the collaboration process was often chaotic and the result was never as perfect as Maysa wanted it to be.

"Maysa, are you okay?" Hydrogen asked, not knowing what she was thinking.

"I—I just—" Maysa stuttered. "I have trouble working with others."

"But your plan might be the only way to defeat Fluorine," Hydrogen replied. "Let's go! Our protons will not be enough." He grabbed Maysa's arm and said, "I know the atom that possesses the most protons in all of Chemistry Land. Her name is Oganesson. She has 118 protons!"

Maysa pictured an image of the periodic table. Oganesson was the 118th element. Maysa could understand why Hydrogen had chosen Oganesson for this plan.

Maysa made a fast decision. Working with others just *had* to work.

"Deal," she said. "So, where can we find Oganesson? What will make her join us?"

"We have to rush to find Oganesson. I think I know where she may be."

Hydrogen and Maysa ran across the street to the elevator bay on the right of the Periodic Table. They went up to the third floor and exited the elevator's silver doors. Maysa looked around and saw several multicolored doors with chemical symbols and the names of elements on them. Fluorescent lights shined down from the ceiling on Maysa and Hydrogen as they made their way to the intersection of noble gasses and newly discovered elements. Maysa looked to her right and saw a purple door with a purple wall bordering it. The letters "Og" were printed on the door, and stenciled above it were the words "ROOM 118."

"Is that Oganesson?" Maysa asked Hydrogen, peering through a small window on the door. Maysa pointed toward a dark blue atom that looked 118 times bigger than Hydrogen.

"Yes," stated Hydrogen, yanking open the door and running toward Oganesson.

"Oganesson! Oganesson!" Hydrogen yelled. "Fluorine is sucking up all the atoms' electrons, and we need your help to defeat him!"

"What are you doing here? What's happening?" Oganesson turned her nucleus slowly toward Maysa and Hydrogen. "Why is Fluorine sucking up all the electrons?"

Hydrogen took a deep breath. "We don't have time to explain the details. Fluorine is about to attack us! We need your help right now."

"What do you need me to do?" asked Oganesson.

"You, Hydrogen, and I must join forces to create a positive field to stop Fluorine," said Maysa.

"But I'm radioactive, so how will you stabilize me?" asked Oganesson.

Maysa blurted out her idea. "Since I was reduced from a human into an atom, I have high energy levels inside me. This means I can ionize other atoms—I can stabilize atoms of radioactive elements by removing a few of their electrons."

"You can do that?" gasped Hydrogen. "How?"

"I think I just need something to anchor me during the ionization process. Hold my hand, and keep holding it, even if I squeeze tight."

Maysa grasped Hydrogen's hand and closed her eyes. She focused all her thoughts on her chemistry set, imagining the joy she felt when she was combining atoms to make molecules. She could feel her nucleus start to heat up, making her light-headed and dizzy. Then the pains began as her electrons bounced chaotically against her atom walls. Neon-red rings encircled each of Maysa and Hydrogen's hands, gradually getting larger until they formed concentric circles around their nuclei.

Then, suddenly, *ZAP*! A neon-red starburst shape enveloped Oganesson, who looked frozen in shock. Oganesson was now ionized and ready to battle. And just in time—as Fluorine was approaching the right side of the Periodic Table Building.

Maysa began to panic. "I don't think we're going to stop Fluorine in time! What if he snatches our electrons before we can get our plan in motion?"

The three quickly dashed out of Oganesson's door, went down the elevator to the first floor, and ran out the building's front exit.

"Uh-oh," said Oganesson, looking at Maysa. "We better get in formation."

After taking a deep breath, Maysa stepped in the middle of the line Hydrogen and Oganesson were forming.

Fluorine had expanded even further, now resembling an immense, acid-green cyclone. His eyes narrowed as he spied the three. Fluorine crept toward them, his cloud tentacles swirling and ready to snatch their electrons.

"*Aha!*" Fluorine snarled. "Precious electrons, waiting for me!"

His cloud tentacles reached toward the outer shells of the three, about to grasp a handful of electrons.

Maysa, Hydrogen, and Oganesson quickly arranged themselves in a defensive triangle position, with Oganesson and Hydrogen as the two bottom corners and Maysa floating up top. Neon-red rings of positive energy encircled each of the three, connected by lines of positive energy to form a triangle shape.

"Not so fast, Fluorine!" said Maysa angrily. "You know how atoms feel when you steal their electrons!"
Hydrogen powered his proton up. Oganesson powered her 118 protons. Lastly, Maysa powered hers, shouting, "Emit positive force now!"

"*YAHHHHH!*" the three shouted together.

Everything was tinted a bright red as the positive force burst out of their nuclei, almost blinding Fluorine. The positive force blew Fluorine back toward the Periodic Table Building, crashing him against the wall. His green gas cloud gradually dissipated as the electrons Fluorine had taken got knocked out of his outer shells' orbit.

"W—what? *NOOOOOO!*" screamed Fluorine.

The electrons Fluorine had stolen rolled across the ground, color-coded for each atom to which they belonged. Maysa, lying flat on the ground from the force of the reaction, watched as the electrons rolled toward their atom owners. The electrons were automatically pulled to their owners' outer shells and magnetically clicked into their orbital path.

The atoms slowly got up off the ground, delighted to be made whole again. Maysa smiled. Success!

Meanwhile, Fluorine shrunk down to his original size and sat forlornly on the curb.

"I'll never get the respect I deserve in Chemistry Land!" wailed Fluorine. "All I wanted was for the other atoms to know I could do more than make toothpaste."

As Maysa watched Fluorine, she almost felt sorry for him. She glanced at Hydrogen and Oganesson, who were just beginning to stir awake after the reaction.

"Hydrogen, Oganesson, are you okay?" Maysa asked.

"I'm fine—what happened to Fluorine?" asked Hydrogen as he rubbed his eyes from the daze.

"Look around, the plan worked!" Maysa said.

"Do all the atoms have their electrons back again?" Oganesson asked, still dazed.

Before Maysa could respond, all the other atoms began to applaud for Maysa, Hydrogen, and Oganesson. The three clambered to their feet and joined in the clapping to show their excitement.

"It took all three of us to beat Fluorine," Hydrogen whispered into Maysa's ear.

"Working together," Maysa added.

The now familiar sparkly pink and blue light spiraled in circles in front of Maysa. The spiral kept enlarging until, with another poof of glittering gold dust, the portal that Maysa had magically gone through at the start reappeared.

"Look, there's the portal!" she said to Hydrogen.

"The portal only appears when it's time for someone to enter or exit Chemistry Land," said Hydrogen. "Since it knows that all the atoms have been saved, it's inviting you to go home now."

"Really?" asked Maysa. "But I sort of feel like I want to stay for a little while."

"You can come here whenever the portal appears for you," Oganesson chimed in.

"Come on. I'll lead you to the portal exit," Hydrogen added.

"Bye, Maysa!" said Oganesson.

"Remember the awesome things you can do if you work with others!" said Hydrogen, standing by the portal.

"Okay ... bye, Hydrogen! Bye, Oganesson! I'll never forget this experience!" said Maysa.

And with that, she transported. Maysa walked out of the portal and found herself back in her living room. As she looked down at herself, she realized her body had returned to its normal size. She wasn't an atom anymore. And she wasn't the same Maysa anymore, either.

WHAT IS FLUORINE?

Fluorine is a halogen on the periodic table with the chemical symbol F and atomic number 9. Halogens are very reactive elements located in group 17 of the periodic table. Bonding-wise, because halogens always have one electron missing (keeping them from being stable), they always want to borrow an electron from another atom.

Fluorine is the most reactive element in the halogen family and on the whole periodic table. Talk about an element with an attitude!

Fluorine appears as a pale yellow gas at room temperature. Use-wise, you may recognize fluorine compounds (also known as fluoride) in your toothpaste. But fluorine can do much more—it can also produce nuclear power and energy!

Just how do you keep this element's power in check? With calcium! Remember when I said earlier that fluorine can be used in toothpaste? Well, in your body, calcium can remove fluorine compounds from your teeth and bones, which is bad for your health. But when you're eating, it's iodine (another halogen) that beats fluorine. *Hyah*! Neutralized. Take that, fluorine!

HOW NEON AND KRYPTON GOT STUCK TOGETHER

(*Forever*. Again, Not Real.)

Remember Maysa? That girl in my story, *Saving the Atoms,* who—saved the atoms? From Fluorine? In Chemistry Land? (See page 79 for the story.)

Well, in *The Neon Sign*, the story that starts on page 99, Maysa is now a teenager. You heard me right— she has new clothes, she's in a new school, and now she and her mom have set up a diner business. But she still loves chemistry and has a special power that lets her talk to atoms.

On top of the diner is a neon sign. Inside the tubes of that neon sign live two atoms, Neon and Krypton. But how did they end up here together? Let's uncover this mystery as we pick up where we left off from *Saving the Atoms*.

Neon and Krypton first lived in Chemistry Land, the place Maysa visited through the portal. During the Fluorine crisis, Neon and Krypton both had some of their electrons stolen. They only caught a glimpse of Maysa defeating Fluorine. But when everyone got their electrons back, Neon and Krypton took a good look at Maysa and recognized the role she'd played in saving them.

Several years after Maysa exited through the Chemistry Land portal, another problem arose. Fluorine got jealous and greedy again, so he and the other halogens teamed up to take over Chemistry Land. Just like Fluorine, Chlorine, Bromine, Iodine, Astatine, and Tennessine felt underappreciated by their atom peers, so they tried to steal ALL the electrons in Chemistry Land.

The halogens combined were much more powerful than Fluorine alone. Krypton and Neon knew the halogens were going to steal all their electrons, so the two atoms had no choice but to flee Chemistry Land. But not just to any place. They escaped to Maysa's place because they knew she would protect them.

Neon and Krypton exited Chemistry Land and looked for Maysa on Earth. Searching for the girl was akin to solving eight Rubik's cubes with your feet. But they finally found her and took refuge in the neon sign of the diner that Maysa and her mother operated.

Neon and Krypton felt they were in a safe place. Together. Forever.

Until something happened to that neon sign … read on, to find out more.

THE NEON SIGN

(A Krypton Story)

Dark clouds crowded the cold night sky, framing the flickering sign. Its green neon light used to glow brightly, with five letters that spelled "DINER." But now, only the "D" and "R" shone intermittently, while the "INE" had fallen dark. The diner itself had become equally shabby. The red and white awning was fading, the leather on the booths was peeling along the edges, and the windows were tinged with the dust of time.

With each passing day, fewer customers visited the diner, its fortunes following the same ruin as its sign. Three new eateries had opened along the block over the past years, their interiors and exteriors modern and inviting to passersby.

Two sluggish noble gas atoms, Krypton and Neon, lived inside the sealed glass tubes of the neglected sign. Their round nuclei lay flat, arms and legs splayed by their sides. They could barely generate enough energy to move or converse with each other.[5]

"Only two customers visited the diner tonight," whispered Krypton glumly.

"Such a sad situation," responded Neon.

"If only Maysa and her mom would fix our sign . . . we would shine brightly and customers would once again visit the diner," said Krypton wistfully.

"It has been two months since our sign worked properly. We have been forgotten," lamented Neon.

---

[5] To learn how neon signs light up, see page 123.

Then, the two atoms heard the faint voices of Maysa and her mother as they locked the diner's doors for the night.

"Maysa, I'm afraid we will have to close down the diner," said her mother softly.

"Oh no, why?" Maysa asked, her eyes widening in alarm. She loved helping her mother make the delicious pizza bruschetta and knew that her mother's sweet blueberry crumble was supreme.

"We don't have enough customers, and we will run out of money by the end of the month." Her mother's voice broke as she told Maysa the truth about their bleak financial situation.

Tears glistened in Maysa's eyes, rolling slowly down her cheek as she contemplated life without the diner. Maysa's mother hugged her tightly as they stood in front of the diner's entrance. Thoughts spiraled in Maysa's head like a hurricane had just unleashed, spreading panic and worry across her body. Her breath quickened, and her stomach felt as if it was tied in a knot. If the diner had no customers, she and her mother would have to shut it down for good. How would they be able to afford their rent? Or buy food to eat? Or pay her cellphone bill?

Maysa stared up at the diner sign and was suddenly struck by something that other girls her age wouldn't notice: a neon sign is comprised of two atoms, Krypton and Neon.

Years before, Maysa had been transported to a place called Chemistry Land, where all atoms live and provide humans with the chemical compounds they use every day. At the time, Maysa was helping Hydrogen and Oganesson to overcome Fluorine from stealing other atoms' electrons. What if she could now connect to Krypton and Neon, and then find a way for them to fix the sign?

Maybe, just maybe, more customers would then come to the diner.

"We could just fix the sign!" Maysa blurted to her mother. "Then people will know we're here and visit the diner."

"But, sweetie, fixing the sign will cost a lot of money." Maysa's mom sighed. "Any money we have should go into making the food for the diner."

Maysa considered her mother's response. Maysa had to try to communicate with Krypton and Neon so they could fix the sign themselves. It just might work!

Maysa squeezed her eyes shut until her brows furrowed, trying to project her thoughts and feelings to Krypton and Neon. The tornado inside her head whirled, lifting upward to the sign until it reached the two atoms.

Krypton and Neon had been watching Maysa and her mother in dismay while the wind whistled loudly around the sign. Black storm clouds began to form in the distance. The two atoms now felt a tingling inside them from Maysa's distress about the diner's plight. Maysa had once saved Chemistry Land, and now Neon and Krypton felt a duty to help her in return.

"Do you think that we *could* fix the sign ourselves?" ventured Neon.

"But how? We've been stuck in this position for the last two months!" said Krypton.

"If we somehow manage to collide by moving toward each other, we possibly could create energy and the sign would light up," Neon explained.

"But how will we collide?" asked Krypton.

"Let's just try to push toward each other and see what happens."

Krypton nodded in agreement. The two atoms tried to roll toward each other. They strained as they pushed their arms and legs against the tube walls, grunting with effort. But no matter how hard they tried, neither of them budged.

"It's no use," panted Neon with a ragged breath.

"I know what we need," declared Krypton. "An electromagnetic field of some sort."

As they pondered their plight, the storm clouds grew closer and thunder rumbled in the air. The night had now taken an angry turn. A lightning bolt cracked the sky, a signal that a storm was soon to unleash. It simultaneously unleashed an idea in Neon's mind.

"That's it!" exclaimed Neon, pushing his hand against the tube wall. "If the lightning hits the sign, it will create an electromagnetic field!"

Krypton's eyes widened at the possibility. "Do you really think that could work?"

Krypton and Neon stared at each other, excitement building at the prospect of escaping their lethargic state.

Krypton and Neon lay in wait as the storm's eye grew closer. The lightning bolts were coming faster and stronger now, dazzling the sky until the storm's eye was above the diner. And then it happened. Lightning struck!

Inside the sign, the two atoms jolted to life. They bounced around the tubes like two small balls, which made the energy levels of both atoms rise. They began hurtling toward each other, their imminent collision inevitable. Krypton burst upon impact, radiating waves of vivid green light.

Sparks flew inside the tubes like a fireworks display. Meanwhile, Neon's energy was spent as he lay ionized from the reaction. Neon and Krypton caught each other's eyes, feeling a mix of pride and relief.

All five letters of the DINER sign shined brightly once again. Krypton and Neon high-fived.

"We've got Maysa's back," Krypton whispered.

"Always," Neon replied.

Krypton and Neon spent the rest of the night sleeping inside the sign, comforted by their accomplishment and the easing storm.

———

Early the next morning, Maysa and her mother arrived. Maysa excitedly pointed at the now glowing neon sign.

"Mom, look! The sign's working again!" she exclaimed.

"How is that possible?" asked her mom incredulously. "We didn't fix it."

Maysa smiled on the inside. She once again projected her thoughts toward Krypton and Neon. *I'm so grateful to you both for fixing our sign! Maybe we'll be able to save the diner after all!*

Maysa turned to her mom. "I think it's a sign that our sign is working," she said, tightly embracing her mom.

The two then entered the diner, excited to make a fresh start to the day. Several family recipes flashed through Maysa's mind. *I want a dish that could bring people of all ages together*, she thought. *Maybe something that people can't resist the smell and taste of!* She finally landed on one: her special family margherita pizza.

"Mom," said Maysa, "could we make our special pizza family recipe, please? Then people would see that our food is better than any other restaurant's on the street!"

"That sounds like a great idea. Let's make some pizza!"

"Yes! Thanks, Mom!"

The two got to work, mixing and rolling the dough, spreading the mozzarella cheese over the fragrant tomato sauce. When Maysa's mother took the pizza out of the oven later, the two were overwhelmed by the irresistible smell of garlic, paprika, and tomato combined with melty cheese.

"I think it smells amazing," declared Maysa.

She opened the diner's windows so that the pizza smells would waft outside, and then walked to the door, turning over the CLOSED sign so then it read OPEN. Maysa spied a couple passing by the diner. They seemed to have noticed the OPEN sign and entered the diner.

"Do I smell ... fresh margherita pizza?" the woman eagerly asked.

"Yes, you do! Come on in!" Maysa greeted them, showing them to a table.

Three more customers followed, also attracted by the irresistible smells.

Maysa hurried to the kitchen to plate slices of pizza for their customers.

"Mom, I think we just opened a new chapter," Maysa whispered.

Her mother gave her a quick hug. "I think there's hope for the diner after all. I'll serve the pizza to the customers. Can you set the tables outside, please?"

Maysa walked to the sunlit sidewalk, tablecloths draped over her arm. She took a few extra steps so she could look squarely at the neon sign above the diner. She gave a thumbs-up as a signal to Neon and Krypton that the plan had worked.

"The diner has customers again!" said Krypton, beaming.

"Looks like we've got great team *chemistry*!" responded Neon with a sly smile.

"You and your *cheesy* puns, Neon," sighed Krypton. Then she added, "I sure hope our diner customers have a positive *gut reaction* when eating Maysa's pizza!"

PART TWO

Cool Chemistry Concepts

HOW DO YOU READ THE PERIODIC TABLE?

The periodic table may look complex, but there are only two important things to really understand:

First, the elements are ordered by their weight, or *atomic mass*. That means that the lightest elements are at the start, and the heaviest ones are at the end. For example, hydrogen (the first element in the table) is the lightest element. Oganesson (the last one) is the heaviest.

Second, the elements are organized by rows and columns. Altogether, the periodic table has eighteen columns and seven rows. This is why it is called a "table."

Each row, or *period*, starts with a shiny metal, like sodium or potassium. Then, it moves onto transition metals that can conduct electricity, like copper, nickel, or iron. Next up come the semimetals, like silicon. Finally come the nonmetals, like oxygen and carbon. The last nonmetal is a colorless, unreactive gas like helium (yeah, like what you use to blow up party balloons). The unreactive gases are like the caboose of a row on the periodic table. This repetitive pattern is why the table is called "*periodic*."

Each column, or *group*, contains elements that have common characteristics. It's like they're all part of the same family. There are ten families in the periodic table, which are often differentiated by the color of the squares. Some families are loud and noisy, while others are quiet. For example, there's the halogen family, which is very reactive to every electron they meet. In contrast, there's the noble gas family, which rarely reacts to anything.

Each element on the periodic table has its own square, which is kind of like a name tag. The square has the element's name, atomic number, atomic mass, and chemical symbol. The atomic number is how many protons are in the element's atom. Every element has a different atomic number. For example, hydrogen's atomic number is 1 because a hydrogen atom has only one proton. The chemical symbol is one or two letters that represent the element. For example, iron's chemical symbol is Fe, and oxygen's is O.

HOW AND WHY DO ATOMS BOND?

Atoms always like to be stable. But how do they get stable? They combine with other atoms. They take, give away, or share their electrons with other atoms, to be exact. This process of pairing up electrons is called *bonding*.

Atoms have circular shells. The electrons orbit on the shells, like how cars drive on a highway loop. The electrons on the outermost shell are called *valence* electrons. For example, oxygen has two shells: an inner shell with two electrons and an outer shell with six electrons. The outer six electrons are valence electrons. Valence electrons are the only electrons that form bonds with other atoms.

In chemical bonding, eight is your magic number. The main goal for bonding is that each atom has to have eight valence electrons in its outer shell. If an atom has a full set of eight electrons, then it is stable. Because all the noble gases are stable, they all (except helium) have eight electrons in their outer shells. Try to count how many valence electrons each oxygen atom has in the illustration on page 117.

When two or more atoms bond, they form *molecules*, like the oxygen molecule, which is two oxygen atoms that bond together. Molecules could combine into more complex structures with different elements called *compounds*. A compound you might've heard of is the water compound: H2O. Water has two hydrogen atoms and one oxygen atom in it. All compounds are molecules, but not all molecules are compounds.

If you were to imagine that you're an atom and your family is an element, you could think of a compound as making friends with someone not in your own family.

 **= VALENCE ELECTRON**

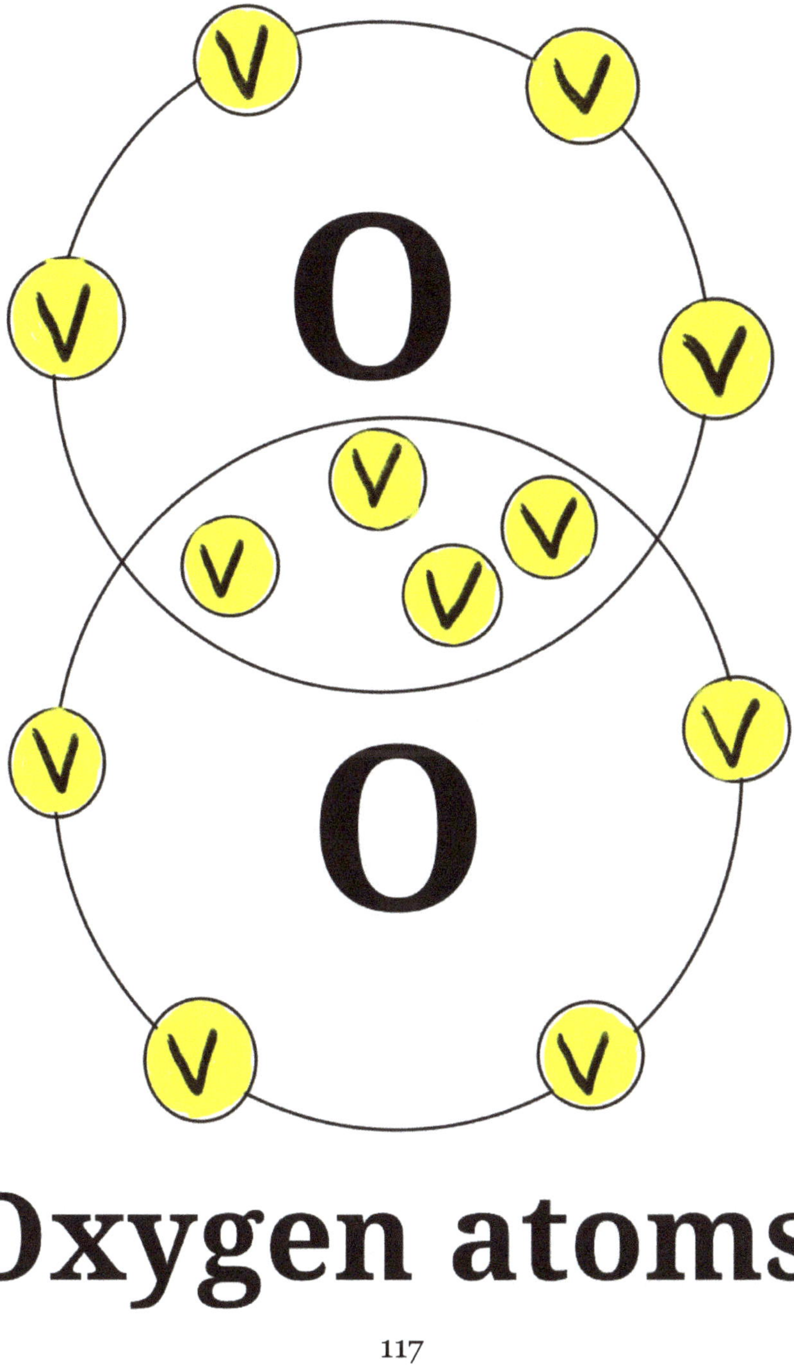

O

O

Oxygen atoms

WHO WAS DMITRI MENDELEEV?

Dmitri Ivanovich Mendeleev (men-dul-LAY-yuh) was a Russian chemist who invented the first version of the periodic table.

In the 1860s, Mendeleev was writing a chemistry textbook called *The Principles of Chemistry* when he made a discovery that would change the field of chemistry forever: different families of elements had things in common with each other in how they behaved.

Mendeleev ordered all the elements that were known in his time by atomic mass and atomic number into a grid-looking chart. By using this new system, he could predict what characteristics elements that haven't been discovered yet would have. He presented his discoveries to the Russian Chemical Society in 1869 and taught a lecture called "The Periodic Law of the Chemical Elements" in London in 1889.

His periodic table of the elements remains an icon in chemistry to this day. Now, many chemistry classrooms have a poster of the periodic table on the wall, and chemists use the table to predict the properties of undiscovered elements, just like Mendeleev did. There have been various changes to the periodic table's organization and shape. But let's all appreciate this glorious chemical list the way it is today—and the professor who started it all.

Dmitri Mendeleev (1834-1907) created the periodic table by observing patterns, or trends, among the elements.

HOW DOES A CYCLOTRON WORK?

While elements cannot break down into smaller things, they can be combined to make new elements. But how?

Scientists make new elements by taking existing elements and fusing them together. This process combines the protons of the fused atoms. For example, if you fuse an atom of calcium, which has 20 protons, with an atom of curium, which has 96 protons, you get an atom of livermorium, which has 116 protons. Simple addition.

But there's just one problem with fusion: the atoms have a lot of positive energy, so they don't want to combine naturally. Think of two magnets that are facing each other with the same pole—they repel. To overcome this repelling force, scientists use a machine called a cyclotron.

A cyclotron is a particle accelerator, which shoots one element at another element by a beam. Take the bismuth and krypton example I use in my story entitled *Who Is Element 119?* (see page 11).

Krypton has 36 protons, and bismuth has 83. Those are also the numbers my characters named Bismuth Beth and Krypton Kate have on top of their heads. In the cyclotron, the element with fewer protons (krypton, in this scenario) accelerates around two large D-shaped magnets. The krypton goes faster and faster in a circular orbit until it gets close to the speed of light. Once the speed is fast enough, the krypton can finally be blasted by the cyclotron onto the target (bismuth, in this case.)

You can say good-bye to that repelling force the elements had before, because now the two existing elements can fuse together into a new element. In this case, that element is … ununennium.

HOW DO NEON SIGNS LIGHT UP?

A neon sign is a glowing invitation that you might see on top of a building or someplace else on the streets. If neon signs could talk, they'd probably say, "Hey, there! Come on in! See what's going on here!"

But how *do* neon signs attract people? How do these signs glow so brightly?

Well, neon signs are made of multiple glass tubes that are bent into different shapes to form letters and pictures. On one end of a glass tube is the *cathode*, which is positively charged. The other end has an *anode*, which is negatively charged. (Think of the positive and negative sides of a battery. These positive-negative sides help balance the charges.)

What's going on inside the tube of a neon sign? You can't see them, but there are many neon atoms zipping and zooming around like flies (if you've ever seen a fly in your house.) Neon atoms have ten electrons each—two in the inner shell, and eight on the outer one. When a neon atom comes face-to-face with electricity, the eight valence electrons get excited.

Not the feeling you get when you just can't wait for something like a birthday party, but *chemically* excited. This means the valence electrons absorb the electric energy and jump up one energy level.

After a while, those valence electrons lose their energy (it's like when you get bored) and jump back down to their original energy level. This releases the absorbed energy into what we call—light!

Despite the name, neon isn't the only gas you can use in a neon sign. Different noble gases glow different colors. For example, neon glows reddish-orange, helium glows pink, and xenon glows blue.

No matter what noble gas is used in a neon sign, it's sure to be bright. Every time you look up in a busy city and see a glowing invitation overhead, remember that the zipping, zooming atoms in the glass tubes will be looking back at you. (At least, that's how *I* see it …)

ACKNOWLEDGMENTS

I am grateful to the Society of Young Inklings for providing me with a vibrant community of youth writers, as well as to Elizabeth Verdick for her mentorship and encouragement in my creative writing. I appreciate my sixth grade science teacher, Ms. Labriola, for always making science fun. Lastly, I thank my mother for her partnership, coaching, and motivation.

ABOUT THE AUTHOR/ILLUSTRATOR

Maya Mourshed is in seventh grade and lives in Maryland. She likes science, math, art, poetry, and music. Maya plays the piano and is learning to speak Spanish. In her free time, she enjoys drawing, writing poems and short stories, and composing mashups, songs, and raps. She wants to continue combining diverse disciplines, like chemistry and music, as she grows up. Maya is currently working on another short-story and poem anthology—this time about math.

www.ingramcontent.com/pod-product-compliance
Lightning Source LLC
Chambersburg PA
CBHW050443150626
46551CB00028B/1208